SPEECH

AND POWER OF EXPRESSION

On Language, Esthetics, and Belief

SPEECH

AND POWER OF EXPRESSION

On Language, Esthetics, and Belief

M. Fethullah Gülen

Translated by Korkut Altay

New Jersey

Copyright © 2010 by Tughra Books

Originally published in Turkish as *Beyan*, Nil Yayınları, Istanbul, 2006

13 12 11 10   1 2 3 4

Published by Tughra Books

345 Clifton Ave., Clifton,

NJ, 07011, USA

www.tughrabooks.com

Library of Congress Cataloging-in-Publication Data Available

ISBN: 978-1-59784-216-7 (Hardcover)

ISBN: 978-1-59784-229-7 (Paperback)

Printed by

Çağlayan A.Ş., Izmir - Turkey

CONTENTS

PREFACE

The All-Merciful. He has taught the Qur'an.
He has created the human; He has taught him speech.[1]

Nun. By the Pen and what they write with it line by line.[2]

The question as to why there is evil in the world has always boggled the mind. Some may be seriously searching for an answer. However, as far as this question is concerned, one part of our souls seem to echo the skeptical side of our nature, which inclines us more towards doing away with responsibilities. Fire is not evil as long as we use it responsibly. Water is a mercy, but if we build our houses upon a riverbed, then we leave ourselves vulnerable to a deadly flood. Just as it is possible to use a knife to carve out of wood a magnificent piece of art, it can also be used as a weapon to destroy yet another work of art, such as the life divinely breathed into our bodies. Speech is just such an instrument, given on all the face of the earth exclusively to humankind. The range of its power can extend in opposite directions, one as far as to revive a mortified soul, the other as deadly as to start a war.

> *There are words that stop a war*
> *There are words that heal a sore*
> *There are words that just render*
> *A poisonous dish a delicacy*

> Yunus Emre

Aware of this power, Arabs viewed poets as akin to soothsayers and thought they had connections with the spirits. When they

---

1   Qur'an, 55:1–4
2   Qur'an 68:1

heard the Qur'an for the first time, Meccans of the Age of Ignorance were mesmerized by the power of its words. Yet, blinded by
disbelief, they reduced the Prophet to a poet; they were as far distant from the divine as a community could possibly be. Although
they were captivated by the Qur'ran, they believed it was sorcery
and thought that it should be ignored. But when poets such as
Hansa and Lebid embraced Islam and subsequently abandoned poetry out of respect and awe of the Qur'an's style and eloquence, the
unbelievers had to confess: "If we call it a piece of poetry, it is not.
If we designate it a piece of rhymed prose, it is not. If we describe
it as the word of a soothsayer, it is not." At times, they could not
help listening to the Prophet's recitation secretly at night; even so,
they could not overcome their arrogance long enough to believe in
its Divine origin.[3]

The book in your hands is about this unique art of speech and
it comes from a master of this skill. While Fethullah Gülen is revered by many for his authority as a scholar and for his achievements in education and dialogue, his power of expression and oratory skills should earn him equal renown. His impact on anyone
who has happened to listen to him directly or through an audio re-
cording is primarily because of his excellent oratory abilities, combined with a message that is acceptable to all—an ideal combination
the components of which cross-fertilize one another to accomplish
the objectives aimed in both. With the exception of misinformed
sections of our society, polls show that a great majority supports his
sincere message advocating peace, promoting education, reaching
out to the poor and condemning terror and violence in all its forms.
He has dedicated his entire career to teaching the God-given dignity of humans and all existence, while encouraging believers to self-
lessly engage with others without forsaking due reverence to re-
spective positions, values, and identity, and by "reserving a seat for
all in their hearts."

---

[3]   See M. Fethullah Gülen. *The Essentials of the Islamic Faith*, NJ: Tughra Books, 2006,
       p. 223-4.

For Gülen, nothing in the world is in vain; such is also true of speech. He echoes the Qur'an in this sense, in which glad tidings of paradise are given to believers who *"will hear therein neither vain talk nor falsehood"* (78:35). Thus, we always find in Gülen's writings and speeches a conscious orientation of the theme towards what he calls the "conversation of the Beloved" (*sohbet-i canan* – [*sohbat al-janan*] in Gülen's words) or an effort to revive in his audience awareness of our servant-hood to God and of our duties towards humanity and the world.[4]

"One feels as if standing on the side of a waterfall"[5] when he listens to Gülen. His sermons, effervescent with love and submission, have the potential to move thousands, but not in a firebrand style. He is always cautious when he addresses an audience, for he is well aware of the command one can administer over masses by "rhetorical persuasion" frequently utilized for evil ends in the past.

Gülen has commanded distinguished oratory skills from an early age. It is noted in his biography that when he first climbed the stairs to the pulpit, he was "not tall enough to reach over [it]." Enes Ergene explains Gülen's talent in speech and span of influence as follows:

> His public speaking is probably the most outstanding of his many aspects. In fact, many people have come to know him only through his fervent oratory. His knowledge and scholarly interests in Islamic studies and modern Western sciences have been overshadowed for years by his mastery of oratory although his articles and poetry were being published in various magazines. For long years, he studied not only religious fields but also history, philosophy, sociology, literature, and art. However, all aspects of this absorbed knowledge would come to the surface either in molding the masses and trans-

---

4   See the Qur'an 4:84, *"Urge on the believers (to take their responsibility)."*
5   Ali Osman Dönmez. "Hocaefendi'nin Edebiyata Dair Fikirlerini Anlama Yolculuğu," *Yağmur*, 47, March-April 2010.

forming them into "teachers," or in other instances when they
could be put into practice.[6]

With all respect to the growing number of academic research
on Gülen and the movement inspired by his teachings, Gülen's
thought and sources of knowledge have not yet been thoroughly
studied. With essays on language, poetry, woman and mercy, beauty and divine love, Rumi, the Prophet, this book could perhaps
slide the gate a bit further ajar, welcoming us into the vast and deep
lands of knowledge that beam through his words, and will hopeful-
ly provide inspiration for researchers to further explore Gülen.

Translation is an effort to reflect the original text as accurately
and as accessibly as possible in the target language. Especially in the
case of works by scholars such as Gülen, this "effort" is a real challenge and it demands exhaustive brainwork. This book is the fruit
of such meticulous work by Korkut Altay and Erhan Yükselci, who
tirelessly dwelled upon Gülen's essays and did an excellent work in
translating them into English. The essay on Rumi was translated by
Professor Zeki Sarıtoprak and previously published as a Foreword
to *Fundamentals of Rumi's Thought*, an important book by late Şefik
Can; we are indebted to Professor Sarıtoprak for his contribution
with this translation. The text has been inquisitively edited by Ruth
Woodhall and Jane Louise Kandur whose constructive comments
extensively contributed to the editorial process and refined the text
into its present form. We also thank Makiz Ansari and Lee Flamand
who helped with the editing of some of the essays.

---

[6]   Mehmet Enes Ergene. *Tradition Witnessing the Modern Age: An Analysis of the Gülen
Movement*, NJ: Tughra Books, 2008, p. 11.

SPEECH AND POWER OF EXPRESSION

Divine Knowledge has designed the scheme of existence, while His Speech has drawn its architecture.[1] After emerging as twins in the most intimate sanctuary of the unchanging essence (*ayan al-thabitah*), creation and Speech took on physical forms. In creating humankind, the Most Merciful gave us the ability to speak of the human essence, our inner depths, the entire cosmos, and the truth beyond material existence before sending us to the dimension of external existence. In this sense, one can argue that speech was the first drop of ink that flowed from the pen of Divine Power to give life to non-existence. Speech has revealed and displayed the mysterious relation between the Creator and the created.

Humankind is nothing more than a clay mixture of the dust and water of the earth; however, thanks to their repository of knowledge[2] and the faculty of speech, they have been elevated to the rank of vicegerent on this same earth. In a sense, humankind is in a position to speak not only on its own behalf but for other beings (like jinn) as well. It is through speech that human beings have become the addressee of God and it is thanks to this faculty that they can address Him. Just as humans started to speak, things that seem silent and reticent have also begun to speak, and all beings and events, which are lines and paragraphs descending from the highest rank (*mala al-'ala*) have become the voice, wisdom-laden tongue and eloquent language of the latent truth within them, like potent

---

1 "Speech" in this essay is an effort to expound on the following verse in the Qur'an: "The All-Merciful. He has taught the Qur'an. He has created the human. He has taught him speech" (Rahman 55:1–4).

2 See Qur'an, Baqara 2:31 and the interpretaion of the verse "God taught Adam the names, all of them" in Ali Unal, *The Qur'an: An Annotated Interpretation in Modern English*, NJ: Tughra Books, 2008, pp. 25–26.

orators. In times when, in our belief, speech did not exist, all beings were silent, all events were mute, and everything was stagnant. How does each being talk? How do they express themselves? These issues are not easy to understand. What is known to us in this respect is that by means of the faculty of speech bestowed in our nature, facility has been afforded for humans to express and interpret every thing at their discretion. Indeed, speech is our soul in this world of relativity. Each of us is a language in his or her own way, and therefore the *raison d'être* of each language is to be a means of speech. Speech is an instrument by way of which truth is acknowledged as the highest reality and all beings become a musical instrument as if in a symphony, thereby removing the veil over things, enabling them to express themselves. Speech is the key that opens the locks on the doors of the treasury of thought. Speech is the key by which a wide-ranging central move stimulates the periphery. Speech is the throne of humans who have been elevated to the position of His vicegerents and given the authority to rule on the earth. Speech is the pen and the sword of humankind and it is the foundation of their kingdom. Wherever the flag of speech waves, the most powerful armies are defeated and scattered. In the arenas in which speech shouts out, the sounds of cannon balls become like the buzzing of bees. From behind the battlements on which the banner of speech has been raised, the sound of its drums are heard. In the precincts where its march reverberates, kings shake in their boots. The Master of Speech smashed to pieces many insurmountable walls, in the face of which Alexander the Great, Napoleon, and many others despaired or retreated; and the pen of Speech, imparting surrender and compliance, was saluted and praised.

THE QUR'AN

The Holy Qur'an is a sample of Speech such that its voice is heard beyond ramparts and echoes in even the most obstinate and bigoted of hearts. There is such dazzling magic in the presentation of its themes that it is impossible not to be impressed upon hearing it.

The expressive style of the Qur'an is like no divine or worldly expression. The Qur'an has such irresistible power to penetrate hearts that even those who do not speak in its language (that is, Arabic) will be fascinated by the melody of its words.

While providing solutions to various predicaments, the Qur'an presents them in such a manner that everybody, except those who are prejudiced against it, will be enthralled or at least touched by it, and led into profound meditation, so that eventually the Qur'an will conquer their hearts.

The Qur'an, this zenith of Speech, displays in each sentence, every paragraph, and each stop an immense depth in meaning, exquisiteness in style, and spirited musical rhythm that penetrates the soul. With its rhythmical grace, with its remarkable selection of words, concepts, and themes that appeals to all the senses in such a fine and cohesive manner that its listeners are transported to wondrous horizons, with surprises of varying degrees of elation at its every turn.

If you attempt to replace the materials the Qur'an uses to discuss a subject, the attempt will be futile, the message will be obscured, and the vivid style will lose its spirit.

The Qur'an has such lofty power of expression that it exhibits different events like living images with their time periods and backgrounds, causing amazement, admiration, and excitement. In doing this, it makes no concessions; nothing detracts from its ravishing beauty, its heart-penetrating profundity, or its phrasal harmony. Rather, it presents everything with clarity, leaving no room for obscurity.

The Qur'an does not only address minds, hearts, or souls. It treats human beings in the totality of their feelings, whether material or spiritual. Its message is brief and concise, but addresses both the inner and the outer world of the person at the same time. The Qur'an generates unity of feeling, thought, and intelligence about the entire universe, all things and all of humanity.

The Qur'an is more influential than the most magical of speeches, more exquisite than the most delicate of styles, and more elevated than the most exceptional of expressions. Up until now, neither those who opposed it with the desire to surpass it nor those kings of eloquence who undertook the task with the urge to imitate it have managed to produce anything that is equal to the Qur'an in speech.

Notable Arab poets, for example Farid al-Din Attar, about whom Shams al-Tabrizi said, "*I might write poems that are sweeter than candy, but I can only ever be his pupil in terms of producing choice words,*" or Rumi, who said, "*I am a bonded servant of the Qur'an,*" or Jami, whom Bediüzzaman described as "*intoxicated by the cup of love*" and their outstanding works, which are still as striking as they were centuries ago, none have ever come close to the Qur'an, the Master of Speech.

We will deal with this issue in detail in future; but for now we will content ourselves with small hints at the narrative style of the Qur'an, and turn back to the reflections which have fallen on our limited comprehension of speech inspired by the Holy Scripture and the verse and prose that develops in its shade.

Through speech have we all had our eyes opened to this world; we have grown up on the lullabies of speech, and those of us who happen to be where they are now have been allured by its magic. Henceforth, our survival depends on speech if we are to live; if we are to die we will die in a drought of speech and knowledge. Speech is the resuscitating breath for living corpses and the water of life for those who want to live forever.

Those who can blow speech over the realm of the spiritually dead, just like a master musician breathing "life" into the flute, will promise resurrection to generations who have been suffering from deprivation for thousands of years, and they will have the effect of Sur[3] on those graves that are afflicted by God's wrath.

If there is a thing most beautiful that keeps its freshness and colors at all times in this guest house of dreams that withers and grows obsolete in every way, in this place where those that have arrived eventually leave and from which those who have settled ulti-

---

3   The Trumpet which the Archangel Israfil will blow to start the Apocalypse.

mately migrate, a place whose property, estates, and pleasures are transient, it is speech. On slopes among which speech echoes, thousands of doves brood in reveries of new rose gardens. As the plectrum of speech strums at the strings of knowledge, objects start to whirl, and events moan as they too whirl to a divine dance. And in those deserts where the echoes of fine speech have permeated, not one, but thousands of Majnuns[4] wander about. Nightingales fall quiet and retire to their nests where streams of the melody of speech are heard. In the wild, where the cries of speech can be heard, foxes take their leave of deception, and lions are terrified, seeking shelter in their dens.

Speech is the spirit, content, color, and pattern of the "book of the Universe" and the laws of creation that are operative in nature; it is the seal, sword, and pen of the truth of Islam as the divine path. In the same way that only goldsmiths can appreciate the karat of gold and only jewelers can appreciate the genuine value of jewels, only wordsmiths can evaluate the actual value of speech. The people of this world can only assign relative values to gold objects or pearls whose lifetime, thus values, are as limited as this worldly life. On the other hand, speech is a king who issues coins at the different levels of the earth and heavens; speech is a commander giving orders and a hero of legends. No person has ever managed to reach the dizzying summits that speech has reached, and no combatant has ever possessed a weapon mightier than speech. Every prophet is a sultan of words, and every person of letters is like those sultans' shadows falling over us. The prophets are the ideals and the people of letters are their followers; the former are architects while the latter are laborers. All of them have acted in cooperation and are united in building prosperous cities from speech, weaving lace from the silken threads of language, and stringing exquisite necklaces with the jewels of words.

When the inspiration of those who wield speech is released, it pours into hearts and turns them into golden pastures which swell

---

4   Majnun is a legendary personality of love found in Islamic literature.

and become fertile in the lush, spring rains, while arid deserts become meadows with the gentle summer showers. And when speech matures and becomes a river, a waterfall, or an ocean which flows in waves, stretching out to the coasts, it attains such an irresistible power that all unseemly voices will be still in the face of its spiritual melody, and all nonsense that pretends to be real words will fall silent, and all talk without content will hide away. A person who is fortunate enough to be nourished by such speech will listen to it; their ego will melt in complete submission as far as they open their heart to it with the intention of intensifying it, as if to allow their soul to be carried into the waterfall of music.

Good speech influences people to the extent of their capacity and potential. Sometimes, encountering a strong gust of speech, people find themselves up in the sky where kites wander, carried up by balloons, and they enjoy the freedom and ease of a bird taking wing in the spacious sky. They are captivated by the allure of speech and start to revolve continuously around that centripetal force. If it were possible for them to stand back and listen to their soul, they would observe what overwhelming feelings of love and pleasure they are wrapped in; they would probably be enraptured. These fortunate people are revived each time they drink from the copious rivers of such sounds and words, discovering themselves anew. As phrases and sentences echo in their ears and downpours into their souls, they experience constant transformations and perceive the magnificence of transcendent life through the colorful dimensions of speech, and are enraptured over and over.

And speech, inspired by the divine and uttered with such feelings and thoughts, entrances listeners with its charm, swirling into their souls and pouring its pigment onto their hearts. They find themselves in the warm bosom of speech, completely surrendering to it. Then, in this comforting atmosphere they can perceive the delights of their own world and lose themselves in the stunning beauty of the riches they are blessed with.

In the gentle murmurs of speech, people sometimes hear the melodies of belief, like the rivers of Paradise, and the melodies of divine annihilation (*fana*) and subsistence (*baqa*)[5]; in the fullness of understanding that all things come from and ultimately return to eternity, they watch with pleasure the ever-changing colors of the horizon of hope and faith.

And sometimes we leave the harbor and set sail to our past, trying to view it in all its magnificence; and sometimes we listen to it, as if it were music, and then dance to it like a whirling dervish and take wing. Entering a state that is beyond time emotionally and spiritually, we find ourselves sitting at the convergence point of past realities and future reveries and observing the three dimensions of time all at once. In this vision, the entire past, which had become a devastated dream, acquires once again all of its earlier magnificence through a wondrous restoration; the future we feel in our beliefs and hopes comes running to us like a joyful child entering our hearts; our longing is subdued and the future becomes ours once again. Thus, with these inner feelings, we submit ourselves to the stream of considerations of all kinds. Inside the tumbling water, to which we have given infinite power and transcendent flow in our dreams, we pass from one state to another, from one thought to another, and just as in our dreams, we shape everything in the pattern that reflects our intent and our state of heart. We cast everything to the mold we aspire and affect them as desired. We can move as we want, taking wing, or landing on the ground to walk when we wish; we can watch the sunrise in the evening or the sunset in the morning; we can increase in number, taking a mere particle and making it into everything.

Speech... speech that nourishes our aspirations which have flourished upon our distinctive foundational essence; speech that sing lullabies to our ideals and taking their feet off the ground to the heavens; such a discerning, sophisticated, and seasoned speech lifts us to the upper reaches of a spiritual ascension and prepares for us thrones in realms beyond the material world. Responding to our desire for eternity, speech enriches our feelings in an indescribable

---

5   See, *Fana fi'llah* and *Baqa bi'llah* in Gülen, *Key Concepts in the Practice of Sufism*, NJ: Tughra Books, 2004, pp. 145–160.

manner and gives our souls a depth that cannot be bound by the dimensions of corporeality; thus we hear the entire cosmos in phenomenal melodies composed without words.

One of the most precious of gifts inherited from our ancestors as a legacy distilled in their hearts, our faculty of speech does not consist only of clarity of meaning, the sound of words, or the expression of certain intentions. It also gives voice to our thoughts, it is the rhythm of our feelings, and the excitement of our hearts; it is the interpreter in our communication with God Almighty and it is the golden-winged turtledove released by our hopes to the future.

Once a refined speech with lofty ideals that comprise all these goals begins to pour out in its own accent, an enunciation which is as expansive as the skies, as full of vigor as the earth, as lustrous as silk, and as comforting as a mother's embrace, it will have a wondrous effect that depicts the awakening of logic, the rampaging of spirits, the charm of words and their journey that stretches to before time. Thus, speech articulates to us the glory of our faith, the riches of our society, the purity and integrity of our fellow companions, the struggle of our ancestors, and our values that make us unique.

Good speech that originates directly from and voices what is in our hearts will always remind us of the breath of the spirit, the beating of the heart, and the color and manner of the faculty of speech. To the extent of the sacredness of its color, wealth and goals, good speech will echo in our hearts like celestial voices providing us with proofs of its origin.

THE POWER OF LITERATURE

In the most general sense, literature is a discipline that studies elegant, measured, and harmonious words uttered or written in verse or prose in a form that is congruent with the conditions of time and usually in compliance with the rules of the language. The Arabic word for literature is *adab*, which has a wider frame of connotation associated with good manners, gentleness, elegance, refinement, and perfection. It has often been interpreted in relation to a person's lifestyle, conduct, and integrity and as a means to the flourishing of that person in spirituality and purification of the heart. In this sense, *adab* falls in the domain of books on ethics or of treatises on Sufism, and therefore it is not usually covered within the discipline of literature. Even so, drawing upon its semantic roots, it is possible to refer to an indirect connection between the two.

Moving on from that relation, I would like to open a small window onto the meaning of literature as I understand it. However, I must first beg that my readers pardon my humble statements on a subject that is in fact beyond my ability, and that they judge this essay not on how it stands, but for the good intentions with which it was written. I should confess that just as I and people like me with narrow horizons cannot judge matters even in our own field properly, so too is it very difficult for us to express other matters very clearly, even when we may have judged them correctly. And I think this is generally true of all who tackle this topic. For instance, after Imam Shafii had personally corrected his book *Kitab al-Umm*, and afterwards still others had repeatedly corrected it, he found that certain points still bothered him. He raised his hands to God and admitted that no book can be faultless, except for divine revelations.

Even the enchanting states inspired by the most magnificent pieces of writing, the greatest works of art, the most eloquent words, and the most dazzling conceptions which are not based on divine speech and are not illumined with the shining of His light have a completely relative beauty. And even if they hold any value in terms of being a reflection or an echo of the beauties He possesses, they can hold absolutely no individual value of their own.

Nevertheless, this reality should never dishearten us or paralyze our determination to work. We should always think, speak, plan, try to realize what we have planned, and while doing all this, we should never forget that we can occasionally make mistakes, that very often we can fall into error. This is natural; as soon as we recognize them, we will correct them, try to compensate for our shortcomings and stick to seeking the best possible alternative.[6] Our decisions may not always be accurate, but we will try to fulfill what divine wisdom requires of us by implementing our human capacity for understanding and judgment (*ijtihad*).

So these humble contemplations must be seen in the same way. In the previous article on speech and power of expression, I tried to explain that speech was born with humanity, developed with humanity, and it constitutes a very significant depth of being human. So speech reached its contemporary level of maturity through history after having been repeatedly distilled through countless filters of thought and fashioned by masters of words, and then became what we now call literature. In this respect, it can be argued that the present moment of literature is brighter than its past, thus it can also be said that so too its future will be brighter than the present, or at least it should be so. As Said Nursi explains, human beings will eventually turn completely toward knowledge (*ilm*) so that they will derive their power from knowledge. As a result the ultimate say will pass into the hands of knowledge. At the stage when knowl-

---

6   The author refers to a theory in the methodology of Islamic jurisprudence, which is called *ashbah bi'l haqq* ("very much like the truth"). According to this theory, when an absolute ruling on a certain issue cannot be found in the Qur'an or in the practice of the Prophet, scholars exercise the procedures in legal methodology and reach a decision with a hope and conviction that their decision is the closest to the will of God.

edge shows such a level of development, the command of language and eloquence, reaching its peak, will outweigh all other values. Possibly, in such a period, in order to make others accept their ideas, people will use language as a weapon, try to penetrate hearts through their facility with language and conquer souls with the charm of literature.

The reality of knowledge and speech manifested only concisely in Adam and it reached its most brilliant form with the Final Prophet, yielded its awaited fruit, and became fully realized in the Qur'an. Now, if the world is going to last any longer, in the years ahead, while knowledge reaches its peak, language too will rise to the rank of the interpreter of knowledge in almost all circles, accompanied by the most powerful of orators and richest of speeches voicing the truth.

The power of expression, which is always nourished and develops in the bosom of need and necessity, will flourish in this environment for one last time, make its voice heard as powerfully as it can. If you will, you could also say this will be the reliving of the Age of the Qur'an in its most mature state, an Age of the Qur'an where love of truth and love of knowledge, where zeal to understand and passion to explain, where human values and their appreciation will live alongside one another. Incidentally, I would like to underline one point: future architects of thought and masters of language should do whatever they can to protect and honor the power of expression, for it has fallen into the incapable hands of people like us. They should untie its tongue, so that it can voice our own world of thoughts. Otherwise, it is obvious that we will keep on hearing the cawing of crows where we expect to hear the singing of nightingales; we will not be able to be free of the distress of thorns on the way to roses.

The power of speech and refinement of eloquence have always developed, found its proper consistency, and come to maturity in the realm of literature and under the tutelage of literary thought. However, it is also very important what we understand—or we are supposed to understand—when literary thought or literature is mentioned.

Human beings have always expressed their feelings, thoughts, and the inspirations of their heart through cinema, theatre, and symbolic painting, along with oral or written literature. When the subject extends beyond spoken or written language, naturally gesture, facial expression, sounds and other means replace words and sentences. Even so, they have never been able to truly substitute for speech and writing. The most reliable way for a people to preserve their literature and make it flourish in its own framework and fertile ground is to put it into a written form. This turns it into a common source to which individuals may refer to at any time. It allows it to become as widely accessible as possible, paving the way for it to become the national style of an entire society, the nation's shared property. It thus becomes a field of exposition for future generations, an exhibition ground of verbal excellence, and a trust to the common conscience, guarded by national memory and perpetuating its own origin.

In this respect, we have always sought literature in the magical world of written or spoken words and always realized our acquaintance and encounters with it among the pages of books and magazines. Whatever style is adopted in recounting a given subject – whether the work produced is approached with an artistic concern or expressed in a plain style, whether a small, select audience is targeted or large crowds are addressed – when literature is mentioned, what comes first to mind is the written word.

It does not make any difference whether the subject of a piece of literature is religion, an idea, philosophy, or doctrine; literature is one of the most important ways that humans can transfer the accumulation of knowledge they have gained through history from one generation to another. Through it they can sense all the depths and richness of yesterday in the present. They see the past and present as two dimensions of reality, and savor the future in its relative depth.

Furthermore, believers should firstly be faithful to their heritage and refer to it frequently, as much as they embrace universal human values. They should emphasize the essence of their common conscience and take it as an essential constituent. They should use this heritage as the canvas for the embroidery in which they depict their literary feelings and understanding of art, so that they do not destroy the spirit of their own literature, and are not constrained solely to foreign borrowings. If they use their own sources and weave their own cultural values on their own loom, there does not seem to be an obstacle to their progress, and they can walk to universality carrying the interpretations of their own time.

Believers should place the main sources of belief, cultural heritage and memory of universal values, in the center of their lives. Thus after having secured themselves from deviation, believers should strive to establish connections with the outside world; remaining indifferent to others' values restricts what is normally broad and universal, is an obstruction to growth, causing agony for the living, and falling from the degree of being envied to a state of envying others; the condition of Third-world countries today presents so many living examples of that.

These countries always go through a period of standstill in their literature, sometimes due to customs, sometimes because of the influence of local understandings, and sometimes due to a fear of self-alienation—which can be empathized to a certain extent. Approaching literature liberally to a large degree ceased due to excessive reactions; some very important sources of inspiration were dried up, and efforts to enrich literature were perceived as fantasy and subsequently dismissed. Moreover, the field of literature was further narrowed at certain times by favoring a region or dialect at the expense of other varieties of the language; the branches with potential to develop were cut off and the roots were removed by prohibiting the field of literature from being ploughed. Thus, in such countries, the development of a language that may have been more representative of the wider society was prevented, and instead a dialect on the margins has been preferred over others, and as a result their literature was reduced to the voice of a small minority rather than becoming a respectable representative of literature in the world. This can also be called surrendering to oblivion.

In fact, what becomes dormant, stops growing, and what is not open to developing withers. Whatever is static then topples over. And that which does not give fruit dies. This is not limited to literature; it is true for almost every subject, from religion to thought, from art to philosophy.

Nevertheless, literature does not simply mean playing on words with written or spoken language skills and producing phrases people will like; it means making the art of expression lovable with the dimensions of eloquence and clarity. It is the water and air of feeding, adorning, and enriching daily language with the cleanest, purest, most lovable, and lasting material, and it is a treasure which increases with use.

A writer of verse or prose who pens his or her thoughts with literary considerations always relies upon a purpose and overtone; using a rich vocabulary, harmonious statements, and a grand style, writers activate words, long and short, aiming for excellence of expression. While moving toward this aim, writers place all the words or sentences they have picked and fitted in their places in such a way that they all sound out like notes serving to support the general theme of the tune they play. As these sounds and notes voice their intended ideal, they continue to play in the background, reflecting the author's mode of thinking, general tendencies and mood.

In a lyric verse, produced by a master of expression the words, feel as if they are filled with that person's excitement. The words, sentences, or lines, springing from a literary heart kindled with epic feelings, ring in our ears like the march of a glorious army. All the words in a masterfully written drama resonate in the depths of our soul and almost bring to life the story therein. A literary person is able to think very differently and reach different judgments; writers always pursue quality and strive to leave future generations a legacy they will gladly inherit and respect.

Actually, like literary language, daily language also has its own kind of beauty, ease, allure, and naturalness that entices pure pleasure. However, literary language is poetic, musical, and constructs a pleasing whole in harmony with the meanings it holds. It is superior in linguistic utilization, taste, and refinement in the way that demonstrates coherence within the text as a whole and cohesion between words and sentences. Let alone feeling and savoring these, it is sometimes very difficult for people who lack the aptitude to even understand them.

All that notwithstanding, it is not correct to regard literary style as the language of an upper class or an aristocratic group. On the contrary, even if they cannot penetrate as far as the secondary meanings and connotations suggested by the composition, people of every level should somehow be able to understand, and they should be able to benefit from that source, even if only in a limited way. Thus, in time they will be elevated to a level where they can express their feelings and thoughts more comfortably and gain greater language skills through the expansion of their knowledge. In the meantime, they will consolidate what they already know of language, enrich it by making suitable contributions as far as they can, and add new depths to their horizons of thought.

No matter at what level, the language almost all of us speak today, which has quietly settled in our memories through generations, is to a great extent the fruit of master poets' and writers' concerted efforts that have been adopted by our souls. With the sensitivity of a goldsmith, these masters of expression presented us with the beautiful jewels of expression and necklaces of words that they prepared; thanks to their legacy, we express ourselves through this rich resource to the best of our abilities. Even though not everybody understands the magnificent works they produced and the aesthetic depth in the spirit of those works, all of us have always appreciated them and felt eager for more. For such a level of appreciation one does not need to know the writer's artistic anxiety, power to construct, mental strain, success in planning, nor his or her true value to the extent a skilful goldsmith knows the precious stones.

People have always held the literary artists in high regard, certainly with exceptions. They have applauded these people's efforts, appreciated their labor, and frequently expressed this appreciation by imitating them. Then what falls to literary people is that they put their language skills and artistic talents at the service of the right, good, and beautiful, instead of hurting the souls of the masses—who can be regarded as their apprentices—by describing what is corrupt, or contaminating people's pure thoughts with dirty images, and condemning them to the slavery of materialism with descriptions of carnal desires. According to Bediüzzaman Said Nursi, people of letters need to have high morals and act within the universal codes of conduct prescribed in divine scriptures. He also reminds us of the divine source where the "power of expression" originates from and advises us to duly respect this capacity, which is regarded as an important depth of our humanity.

Literary styles of expression are different than other styles. For example, in scientific writing or speech it is essential to have a sound pattern of reasoning, a systematic thought, well-versed statements, and no mental, logical, and emotional gaps should be left unfilled. Oratory style emphasizes proofs and arguments, maintaining interest and enthusiasm, making occasional repetitions, supporting the narration with paraphrases when necessary, using colorful expression, and enlivening the speech by inspirational shifts without detracting from the main axis. On the other hand, literary style requires a variety of linguistic arts, such as vividness of expression, accuracy of language, beauty of presentation, richness of imagination, the utilization of metaphors, parables, idioms, figures of speech, and allusions—as long as it does not reach the point of excess. Because excess will spoil—as in everything else—the naturalness of language and muddy the heavenly spring of expression, people of sound taste will mostly find it strange. As Said Nursi also expressed, the wording should be as ornate as the nature of the meaning allows. Form should follow content, and while it is being crafted, permission for literary license should be requested from the meaning in order to avoid excess. The brightness and resplendence of style should be given proper due, but the aim and intended meaning should never be neglected. The imagination should be given room to maneuver, but not at the cost of the Truth.

LANGUAGE AND THOUGHT

Language is one of the fundamental dynamics in the composition of a culture. The power of a nation is directly proportional to the power and richness of its language and thought. A perfect command of language and the ability to engage easily in dialogue with others protect a person from outside influence. Language is an important tool for humankind in our efforts to better understand the cosmos and events both holistically and analytically. From every aspect, language plays a defining role in the formation of our culture.

Language is not only a means of speech and thought, it is a bridge with the significant function of bringing the wealth of the past to our day and conveying today's heritage and our new compositions to the future. All of the cognitive, intellectual and scientific reserves and riches of a nation can become eternal only by means of a language powerful enough to embrace this heritage as a whole, a heritage that has descended from the ancestors and taken new forms in the hands of today's generations. The more richly and colorfully a nation can speak, the more they can think; the more they can think, the broader is the span their speech can reach.

Every single society leaves behind what they speak and think today for its validity to be probed, tested, and protected by future generations. In this way, a huge reserve of experience and learning are saved from being wasted; the knowledge and ideas of the past are utilized for the benefit of the present; what was right or wrong in the past is compared with the rights and wrongs of today so that we do not tread the same path and suffer from the same errors. This is valid for all nations of the world; the capacity of a language to express a thought is related to the level of development it has achieved, and a thought can become the instrument by which the language is tuned to this level of development.

If a language has not developed with its inner dynamics to voice the needs of all times, and therefore the users of that language cannot find the words corresponding to certain concepts, then that language is deprived of the support of thought, and its users are doomed to failure. In a time of industrialization, global commerce, and technological warehouses, no one should stay within the limited span of dictionaries in hand or what they hear and learn from the people around them. Otherwise, they will have to remain silent and merely listen to what others have to say—such indifference to the requirements of the modern age leads to disqualification from participation in contemporary societies.

The earnings of yesterday should be conserved as a cultural heritage and utilized today. Historical and social dynamics are the threads with which national ideals should be interlaced. By all means, this should be realized while opening up to tomorrow and embracing the modern age. As a matter of fact, yesterday has passed with all its frame of reference. What is more, reaching out to the future at full speed requires much more sustenance than we can draw from our homes, family, and immediate environment, though they may suffice for practical daily needs.

Failure is the inescapable end of the ill-fated and forlorn ones who are far from facing their era with their own language and thought. Just as important as ensuring language and thought survive is making them a property of the masses. Societies which do not think and speak will find others speak and think on their behalf. Logic is in disposal of the tongue in crowds where there is speech without thought. Those unfortunate ones who cannot put what they think into words are slaves of their incapability.

Although not in great numbers, there are still self-confident thinkers who can elaborate their thoughts. Nevertheless, they too are not free from problems. In many countries, those who look like the elite from the outside are in truth alien to their own society. The majority in their society respond to this elite with an inner opposition for they do not trust them, and their thoughts are perceived as nothing more than mere fantasy and imported views. You find the prose of these intellectuals written in their own language but with the mindset of an alien, and when they have to speak they feel the need to switch to the vernacular of their fellow countrymen; thus they travel in between several worlds in their inner presence, in a state of multiple belongings to different realms at the same time. They cannot adjust their hearts to beat in tune with the heart of their society, nor can they reflect the pattern of eloquence and power of expression embedded in their language. It would be naïve to expect some sort of valuable service from such people who are entrapped in contradictions within their personal world of thought.

For a language truly to become the medium of communication, the overwhelming majority of a society must be able to express themselves in it with full command and reflecting its true nature. Expressions in a complicated way like loading the real intention to diverse allusions or signs and relaying every subject in the form of detailed interpretations are obviously not the most agreeable types of presentation. Language is a phenomenon the worth of which lies intrinsically in itself, like other sciences, and perhaps its importance is even of a greater magnitude. Thus, any society should conceive of its language as a field of knowledge and the interest of the masses must be drawn to it as a pleasurable topic. This is possible only by way of a long list of tasks to do with language: a successful compilation of every single word, a careful study of manuscripts, a deep analysis of the methodology and stylistics of derivative forms in harmony with the peculiar nature of a language, to make widely known and used those words and idioms that have been in use over many centuries, firmly settled with all their nuances, and with their specific meanings revealed best in that language. It is of paramount importance for a nation to be respectful towards all these components of preserving a language. If all these can be achieved, then a language can stand on its own principles and rules, as rich, soft, and amiable as a language can be. Thus, a language can become the lingua franca of an age while maintaining its inherent logic; it will be in use delightfully and will be transferred from one generation to the next. Although this expectation does not seem theoretically or logically exaggerated, it is not easy to realize it; there will be challenges while putting it into practice. Something being logical might not always mean the same thing as the logic of its development, transformation, and maturation—the unfolding of events may follow a different path. In the case of constant change, the logic of development must be given priority above absolute logic, the reins controlling it must be loosed a little, and space for maneuver must be enlarged. If not, language and thought, both living phenomena, will become stagnant, as solidified as rock, and will lose their soul. Language has a determining influence on the national thought and worldview and their logical, intellectual structure. Language has to be in its prime to go beyond historical value and respond positively to every favorable development. Nations that can manage to develop their language and make it accommodating while at the same time staying faithful to the roots of it are the most communicative societies that are also most dynamic in thought.

The relationship between language and thought comprises cognitive and intellectual reflections on existence and events, transforming these reflections into sources of information, and becoming productive while forming links between the cosmos and our knowledge. The future prospects of a nation are very much dependent on evaluating these relationships. We should not cast everything that is old into oblivion, nor turn our face to the past and close our doors to what is new. Let us embrace the past with the utmost sincerity and at the same time salute the coming days with their open, new developments and transformations. Let us not cause any conflict between language and thought, between our past that is filled with exalted memories and our future that we strive so hard for; let us not sacrifice one for the other.

The roots that make up the national spirit should be determined with the help of research. While relying firmly on those roots, a society should endeavor to go beyond them. We should be conscious that revivification is necessary to survive and we must live in order to bear fruit. Our hearts should beat connected to our essential dynamics of our spiritual heritage, and our eyes should be fixed beyond the horizon. We should aim to live and flourish with an insatiable thirst for opening out—this is how it can be possible to make future generations survive, those generations to whose sake we should bind our existence.

It must be those selfless men and women, who are devoted to making others live and expect nothing in return, who cherish this life best with its all possible dimensions.

BEAUTY AND THE BEAUTIFUL

Beauty elevates our hearts, awakens our souls with sweet excitement and appreciation, and then becomes the esthetic of our inner self. This hard-to-describe phenomenon, this sense that is present in our most joyous moments, is beauty. Though this definition might seem narrow, it is one interpretation. There have been many elaborate interpretations of the notion of beauty from the point of view of esthetics, so let us shift our focus here to the relation of beauty with existence, nature, and human beings, and even what is beyond nature.

The meanings of beauty need to be redefined all together in order to be properly appreciated. Although this has been done many times by masters of esthetics, we will try to explain our understanding of beauty in the context of our thought and belief, where every beautiful object is a mirror image or a reflection of Divine Beauty. Anything that incites appreciation, love, and astonishment is a reflection of Divine Beauty and our hearts are filled with these reflections of the everlasting; thus we always consider ourselves absorbed in beauty. Through this perspective, we conceive of even seemingly sad things like death and decay as being the essence of the most amazing harmonies, thus feeling that we are surrounded by infinite beauty. In this way, we never feel upset or discouraged by the fading of our attachments. On the contrary, we experience the outward beauty of faith, breathe in the motivating air of hope, strive to do righteous deeds in the hope that we will fulfill our spiritual desires, seek sincerity in every deed, struggle to be tolerant, merciful, and constructive in all our behavior, and we strive to accept those deeds done for the sake of God as being the best moments of our lives. For us, faith becomes the light that illuminates our horizons, and a source of hope for our expectations. Only through faith can the chaos of nothingness be overcome. Only through faith can we gain the happiness that reaches from our hearts to infinite Paradise. Through its vastness and power, faith becomes beautiful. Through faith one can find Divine Unity, turn toward the Truth, and reach worldly and heavenly bliss, being released from all worries.

These are all the beauties within beauty that can be enjoyed through faith in God. The universe, events, objects, and the human intellect that can appreciate these are all beautiful in that they help us find faith. Likewise, all righteous acts that stem from faith, good morals and the desire to reach real faith and progress in the spiritual ranks of love and knowledge of God are also beautiful. Even acts of worship, or calamities that strike us, or temptations that we find hard to resist, all of which may seem like hardship from the outside, represent beauty if we adopt the right attitude toward them. Real beauty belongs to God. Perfection is exclusively a Divine Attribute, unique to Him alone.

All of existence is a different mirror of God, reflecting His beauty as much as its potential allows. Stars sing of the beauty of light every night, as they twinkle at us and remind us of Him through their extraordinary beauty. Moonlight touches hearts with its softness and beauty, and the sun spreads its mercy on each and every thing without distinction. It pours down its light and colors all day long, and sets, presenting us with another marvelous scene. The seas rise and fall in the tides, and take care of millions of living beings, like a merciful mother. Gargantuan mountains of a size that makes our hearts pound seem to be whispering something to the skies, playing along with the clouds. The mountains invite the rains and hold back the oceans with their proud gaze, yet they crumble away to mere dust and mud. All the voices of the birds, sheep, forests, and mountains make up a harmonious song, feeding our souls with the most peaceful of rhythms.

Yes, everything, from the smiling skies to the thousands of glories of the Earth, is so beautiful that it makes us aware of the beauty of Heaven, and we simply say, "It just could not have been more beautiful!" And human beings themselves seem to be the most beautiful among all this beauty. With our outward looks, our inner world of feeling, thought, and faith, we are like a sample, a replica of the universe. It is therefore apparent that humans have been created as a key to solve the riddle of creation. This is the way we should perceive beauty, seeing it only as a tool to interpret the real meaning of existence. In this enormous arena of beauty, everything can be seen as a point referring to the Creator. If, with pure intentions and the right perspective, we can perceive existence as a mirror reflecting the beauty of the Beautiful, we can experience spiritual joy.

In fact, it should not be difficult to become aware of this. Sometimes, just a beautifully designed city or a place of worship is enough to make us enjoy this holy pleasure. Sometimes, a good poem, a legend, a well-told story, or music that is meant to touch our human sensibilities, that wafts harmony into our soul, can draw us to this beauty and make us hear the beauty of some other abode. However, for the joy of these spiritual pleasures to continue and to avoid suffering we need to relate this worldly beauty to its real Owner. Otherwise, all will end at the most unexpected moment. The Sun will set and the Moon will disappear as our soul sinks into the darkness. It is impossible for souls in decline to appreciate and enjoy beauty. Since every beauty of this world fades away and leaves us one day, for our soul not to despair and to be able to enjoy the real and infinite beauty, it is necessary to establish the true Owner and Originator of the beauty we observe. A poet, relating this concept to a Qur'anic verse said, *"Even faces as beautiful as the Sun set in the end. Thus, I love not ephemeral ones, but the infinite beauty that does not fade away."* Rumi illustrates the same point in the following verses: *"My God, after seeing You, knowing You, I do not see the beauty of this world anymore…"*.

Yes, material beauty is just a means to acknowledge the Most Beautiful. Getting stuck at the "means" and not realizing the ultimate goal of this beauty, which shows us the real Beauty of God, is nothing more than being blind to the real goal, the real Truth. The Creator has placed all sorts of beauty and signs along the way so that we will not be blinded; however, for souls that have not reached this realization and which lack the perspective of faith, this beauty is nothing but a source of mischief, or a means leading them to sin. But for those who can think clearly, even love for the beautifully created is only the shade of the shade of the shade of the Beauty of the Beauty of God. As long as we are able to distinguish between the Real Source of Beauty and its reflection, the love we feel for the created is harmless. In this sense we can accept the created as beautiful.

Sometimes, we are aware of the innermost feelings in our souls which sense only the abstract beauty that fills our hearts with God's love alone. At these moments, when beauty and love become intertwined, the soul, with its unique ability to see, feel, and hear, senses the Real Source in everything that it meets. Through its God-given faculties, our soul perceives the essence of everything and attributes this to its real owner. It is the lack of these faculties that renders materialists and naturalists short-sighted; they only observe the outer beauty of things and fall short of perceiving spiritual and infinite horizons. However, all beauty exists to take us to the Heavens, to the divine realms.

All human beings display themselves, their feelings, and their abilities in their works. This means that they are presenting something to others who will observe and perceive through the prism of their insight. God presents His works embellished with color, meaning, and content in order to make Himself known and loved to those seeking Him. We are sent to this world with the responsibility, then, to affect and reshape things with His permission, to reflect our understanding, but also to be attentive to the true purpose and meaning of the creation of things. The universe and the events in it are thus perfect examples to imitate. However, no matter how perfect the example is, everyone will draw and interpret objects according to their abilities. Charles Lalo, commenting on esthetics once said, that the magnificent scene at sunset would remind a farmer of the rather unaesthetic thought of dinner; the physicist, not of beauty or ugliness, but of the rightness or wrongness of the analysis of a matter. Thus, for Lalo, the sunset is beautiful only for those who are aware of beauty. Therefore, only those who see with God and hear with God can appreciate the beauty that spreads throughout existence as their senses are tuned to the spiritual realms.

A heart that beats with God's love and which desires to meet Him, will be aware of many signs from God along the way. Such a heart will feel the excitement of meeting Him, as it reads the messages from the Moon, the sunset, the twinkling stars, colorful nature, the blowing of the wind, the snow. And such a heart will utter, in the words of one who has reached unity of sight and heart, "Everyone from everywhere is coming to watch Your beauty. From beneath and from above, every being is declaring You, displaying the reflections of Your beauty." This heart looks at nature and objects, but sees the Unseen spiritual realms. This is the point of love and connection with God.

FROM BEAUTY TO DIVINE LOVE

The universe is like a magnificent book adorned with embroidered meanings page by page, line by line, and word by word. It is an exhibition ground of the divine art; it is a palace. All things and the totality of events of every kind in their enchanting harmony, fascinating order, dazzling beauty, and their arrangement and richness more perfect than the best-tended gardens make you say, "There could not be anything more beautiful." All of these constitute an immense and colorful resource for sensible souls to refer to and benefit from. For these souls the universe becomes a poem to be composed with the most immense sensations; those who refer to it are neither tired, nor is that resource or the remarks and stories about it ever exhausted. To put it truly:

> Say: "If all the sea were ink to write my Lord's words (the acts, decrees, and manifestations of all His Names and Attributes), the sea would indeed be exhausted before my Lord's words would be exhausted, even if We were to bring the like of it in addition to it." (Kahf 18:109)

Whenever we turn our gaze from the macro-cosmos to our inner depths, from our scale of human values to the constellations, the meanings flowing into our hearts through different channels of sensation, pluck the strings of our hearts just like a plectrum, its every touch, making our spirits hear such beautiful melodies from the love of Truth. And they make our senses take wing with a thirst for knowledge by waking all our senses to the will to explore. And several times a day, in our consciousness we feel faith turning into knowledge of God; then we feel this knowledge ascend to the horizons of devoted love and joyful zeal, and physical considerations become completely dependent on metaphysical ones. Then a person senses more profoundly that they are becoming completely otherworldly and are reaching into the depths of their own potential, and that many a thing previously concealed is becoming more obvious than the most obvious things. Then they mark their place and position within existence by saying, like Niyazi Misri, *"There is nothing more obvious than God, the Ultimate Truth; He is only hidden to those without eyes,"* and keep proclaiming loudly what divine Providence blessed them with.

Souls so eager for verity and so full of yearning for truth mobilize all their humane feelings and attempt to feel the immense blessings of the One of infinite mercy in a more comprehensive and lucid way. They sense and recognize His Essence through the luminous rays of His Names and see the artful designs of His lacework more clearly and vibrantly in their own inner dimensions. They remain in constant remembrance of Him in a master-slave relationship with the bounteous guidance of the divine favors they are involuntarily blessed with at every moment. As well as constantly remembering Him, they try to express themselves with the consciousness of having gained supreme value thanks to His immense blessings despite their own nothingness. That is, within their own pettiness they proclaim their honorable status and relative grandeur coming from their attachment to God. They use their own impotence and neediness as a key to an otherwise unreachable power and inexhaustible treasure, and then discern and contemplate the fact that there are others who also are aware of this potential. Quite simply, they become experienced divers of their own depths. Later, in proportion to their inner progress and growth, they try to convey every meaning they grasp, and every truth they comprehend and appreciate to others as well. They pronounce their faith in their servanthood to God. They feed their knowledge of the divine through reflection and searching. They transform their interest and curiosity inside into an ever-deepening yearning. All their considerations and observations are pervaded by amazement and appreciation, which they constantly refine with heartfelt gratitude, and they turn their world of feelings and reflections into a waterfall of love of the divine. So they think only of God all the time, walk on in dreams of reunion with Him, and seek Him. They watch out for opportunities to turn to Him and find him. They take every sign as an invitation to start imploring Him again. They orient their life to being in His presence, and whenever they wish to open their mouth and say something, they speak about Him. As well as speaking about Him, they converse with Him almost continuously. We can even say that they sometimes completely become feeling, consciousness, comprehension, and the smiling face of every object offers such beautiful feasts to their senses that they surpass human imagination!

In fact, human beings, who are created on account of God's love for His Essence (*muhabbat al-dhati*), will be acting in accordance with the purpose of His creation only by behaving this way. That is, when God's love for His Essence and His Attributes is manifested in human beings as love for God, then human beings fulfill the purpose of their creation. Thus, everything just fits in its place.

Love is an inner identity, peculiar to humankind among all creatures. They walk confidently toward their own origin and reference with this identity, without becoming entangled in the multiplicities around them. Thanks to the light of the love always blazing deep inside them, they keep watching their target without diverting their gaze, without being distracted by other considerations. We can even say that it is as if they are constantly fixed on their target. Neither impenetrability of meanings, nor greatness of distances can make them hesitate or slip. Although the path of love is so hard and full of sufferings, once having embarked on this path, sufferings turn to pleasure one by one, Mercy overwhelms hardship, and poison turns to sweet honey. And if the eye of the heart thoroughly opens, in every object they see, view, and embed into their hearts, they start seeing the traces, signs, messages, and lights of different frequencies of divine manifestations. Then all the relative lights fade away in from their sight, suns become invisible, moons are eclipsed, and stars are scattered and buried in darkness like prayer beads with a broken string. As the verse reads: *All that is on the earth is perishable, But there remains forever the "Face" of your*

Lord, the One of Majesty and Munificence (Rahman 55:26–27), beyond physical measures, the One and Only God fills the horizons of their hearts. Such a heart, although it is a small thing wrapped in the body, extends to contain its wrapper completely. We can even say that it reaches the capacity of universes in their entirety. So such people constantly feel Him in everything. Interventions caused by their corporeality—which we can compare to lunar eclipses—are as horrifying for them as death and they seek different routes to be able to maintain their awareness.

A person who truly loves God sometimes feels the intersection point of love and reunion so deeply in their world of feelings that everything about the physical world disappears from their sight; they perceive all of existence from one end to the other as torches blazing over the paths stretching before them, pointing beyond the horizons, ablaze. And sometimes, when their yearning is more overwhelming than their hope for reunion, as if holding a hot ember inside, they burn like a furnace and say: *"Even if I burn like a furnace, I do not express any grief,"* (M. Lutfi of Alvar[7])—

Given that no other fire falls into my heart—and they keep on track in a mixed mood of hope and enthusiasm.

As a matter of fact, love is what it is; it is neither simply fire, nor light. Both fire and light are melodies rising from the strings its plectrum touches; both are cries, cheers, and deliriums. Love is such a matchless pearl that only the expert jewelers who have made a bid for pearls at least fifty times in the market appreciate its true value:

> *"Only an expert on jewels appreciates the true worth of a jewel."*
>   M. Lutfi of Alvar

Indeed, one who has not truly loved cannot know what love is, and those who know do not tell or cannot tell. Even if they tell, those who are not in love cannot understand what they say.

Within the frame Providence determines for the lovers, all they can feel is the excited palpitations of their yearning and love for the

---

7   A famous sufi scholar and poet of twentieth century eastern Turkey.

Beloved. Every hue in that atlas is a sign of condescension from the Beloved, every line and every point is a symbol of infinity, and every motif is a call to reunion. Every time lovers gaze on the course of their lives, they say, "O God, I do not know how to express my gratitude that You have created my heart and brought love into existence. Even if I keep following the track for years, like Majnun[8] did, and lie in wait for Your manifestations—my distance from You is a shortcoming of my own. If only I could feel this distance deep within and wander through valleys raving about reunion all the time...." At every object, living or non-living, they say, "This is also a shadow of His light," and wish to smell all of them and holds them so dear. And they strive to feel Him with all of their senses, in every faculty of their being, separately but from a single source. Indeed, this kind of behavior is the only way to fulfill what that pure love requires.

> *The lover who wishes to see the beauty of the beloved in so many faces,*
> *should break into shards, like a shattered mirror...*

> (Anon)

In order to fulfill the requirement of this deathly love, the lover continuously tracks God on the slopes of the heart. He pursues every sound, hue, or sight which he considers as belonging to Him. Sometimes skipping, sometimes crawling, or sometimes flying, but in every station sensing a welcome from Him inside, he puts his eyes at the command of his heart and keeps on tracking as majnuns do. And despite the cruelty of distances, with the most transcendent thoughts he orients all his inward and outward feelings towards being on the path and runs toward the reunion in the realm of the soul. Since he experiences love and union simultaneously, he takes every station as a separate bay of reunion and shakes like a leaf, fearing that one day this reunion will end, and saying, "I neither wish love to end, nor hope, nor the wish for reunion. If one day, the promised reunion will take away all of these, let that not happen either...."

---

8   In Sufi literature, the character Majnun symbolizes an initiate. He falls desperately in love with Layla. In the long run, the initiate's transient love turns into divine love.

What the lover likes is being in love, being on this path, living with the signs and signals of reunion and continuing this flood of feelings forever. Yes, ablaze with the love of the divine, catching fire at every sign of reunion, and while catching fire, being content with this very condition and saying, "The reward is the love itself."

> *This is what true love is!*
> *Look at this poor beggar,*
> *A slave, even to a single strand of the beloved's locks*
> *In the honey of love, I dip my finger*
> *On and on I dip, give me some water!*

Ghedai

A love which is not within this frame cannot be called love in the Sufi sense; it can only be idle gossip about love. Love should not be sought where there is talk about love; it should be sought where flames and embers alternate. For love is an ember secretly burning its bearer from within, or it is such an unbearable condition that when it falls into one's heart, its flame is felt everywhere. It is such a flame that its wick is sheltered by its secrecy. The love which is stripped of its discretion and has become a matter for conversation or a subject for philosophy is not love; it is just a lifeless picture of love. Murmurs of love which take their place in compositions and become their slave are just a reflection of true love, and those narrated in books are just rough definitions. Those who know to keep it concealed in the home of the heart say:

> *If you say you are in love, do not complain about the suffering,*
> *Do not groan and let others know about your groaning.*

(Anon)

They try to keep this inner storm secret, even from themselves. Yes, love is like a dimensionless fire in someone's heart, incinerating everything which belongs to them. We can call it neither heavenly nor earthly. If a heavenly love is for Paradise, then the lover considers it as faithlessness to the Beloved, for worldly love—or metaphorical love as it is called in Sufism—has absolutely nothing to do with true love. Metaphorical love sets its throne on physicality, and all its tricks appeal to the eye; it is considered a deception on the path of love with respect to the balance between what is demanded and its true worth.

True love is a heavenly light or ember which is ignited from the torch of infinity. It transcends the earth and the sky, east and west, and is beyond time and space. Its manifestation is radiance, and there are wisps of peace inside it, giving off the smell of love like incense perfuming all around. Yes, hearts burning with the fire of love keep smoking like an incense holder that makes the scent of the Beloved felt all over the inner world of the lover; and of course, also to their confidants around them who understand the secret. Such people sometimes say,

> *O friend, you have put a burning ember into the ship of my heart*
> *And you call out, "Look, there is a fire on the sea,*

> Suzi

and they try to breathe thus with these inner cries; and sometimes they sound out their suffering on the strings of their heart:

> *O, inn-keeper, I keep burning with the fire of love, give me some water!*
> *On and on I dip my finger in the honey of love, give me some water!*

And they groan at the calls to reunion, but they never refrain from devoting their lives to love; in the eyes of the lover everything other than love is futile, and all cries other than cries of love are meaningless noise.

Love is the most truthful witness of being spaceless within space, and timeless within time. It is a chain of fire lowered from beyond the heavens into the heart of a person, and the people who are bound with this chain are the voluntary slaves of love. Even if they burn, they burn bound with that chain and when they are to die, they dream of dying on the hook of love. They do not consider living without love as life, and they see days which pass without love as autumn leaves drifting on the winds of fancy. Actually, the lover is so merged with spirit that one day, springs yield to autumn, colors darken and laments are sung for the dead. Youthfulness bends double and sits on the benches of the old. All beauties fade like old paintings on a wall and turn into the frames of memories. But that spirit gives fresh life to all other souls. It sets autumn ablaze with the colors of fire; it becomes the elixir of youth against senility and becomes life for spirits which were decaying.

True love is the love which finds its profundity in the immensity of loyalty. If we compare a love which has not yet reached the horizons of loyalty to a good window display of a shop filled with all kinds of riches, then a love which has matured with loyalty can be compared to the valuable stock of a store whose windows are kept closed despite the infinite riches inside. Yes, a love which has not deepened with loyalty is like a stormy sea revealing the churning below, whereas love which has found its true depth through loyalty is like an ocean into which hues or sounds merge and fade away. In the depths of that ocean you neither find a hue nor waves, nor do you hear the sound of churning. Such people are silent as befits their depth and are clear—a clearness which includes all colors within it—as befits their richness, and they avoid all pomp and show in accord with their magnificence.

This very point is where beauty turns into perfect love and becomes a part of one's character, nature and feeling of responsibility; at this point, the integrated harmony, the integrated meanings, and the integrated beauties within existence are distilled through the sensitive filters of feelings, and consciousness, and comprehension combine with the faithful appreciations in the heart; they become a ground for love for God, yearning for Him, and a feeling of being attracted toward Him (*ashq, ishtiyaq, jazba, injizab*). Also, through these powerful relations, the lover devotes his or her entire being to the divine and comes under His command. Rumi expresses this feeling in the following words:

> *I have become a slave, a slave, a slave, a slave...*
> *Slaves feel glad when they are emancipated,*
> *I am joyful and glad for I have become a slave to You.*

Those who do not adorn their faith with knowledge of God cannot avoid spiritual weariness. Those who do not feed their knowledge of God with love for Him get entangled with formalities. And those who cannot associate their love for God with servanthood on the path toward reaching the Beloved One cannot be considered to have expressed their loyalty. Let us conclude with the words of the Sufi saint Rabia al-Adawiya, the great woman who represented a peak of divine love and worship:

> *You talk about loving God while you disobey Him;*
> *I swear by my life that this is a great surprise,*
> *If you were truthful in your love, you would obey Him,*
> *For a lover obeys the one he loves.*

POETRY FROM A HUMBLE PERSPECTIVE

Poetry is the voice, wording, and expression of the truth and essence of humankind, their love, excitement, trouble, grief, and joys, the expression of their sensing and evaluation of existence and the beyond, through the tongue of feelings and emotions in an open or hidden way. From another point of view, we can see it as the heart's feeling of things and events in its own way, feelings' making their own interpretation; a specific evaluation of humankind and the universe with respect to the outward realm and what is behind it by means of the conscience; and the interpreting and sounding out by consciousness and cognition—in spite of their essential functions—of these senses, feelings, and considerations sometimes more or less in conformity with reality, and sometimes in the tow of dreams and imaginings.

Since everyone has their own breadth of conscience, immensity of heart, and richness of feelings, then the depth of their feelings and thoughts, their perspective on things and events, how they interpret what they sense and feel, individual styles, words, and tunes will naturally be different.

Given that some people are unaware of the realms behind visible existence and unable to understand the language of the conscience, some see nothing but material things; since their reasoning is reduced to what they see, and some are ignorant of their own inner worlds, it is obvious that such people will utter lots of sounds and words, whether meaningful or meaningless. Because individuals in any of these groups will voice their inner perceptions, they will reflect the inner picture and plans which form in their conscience, spread in their mind and imagination and then influence their feelings—different beliefs, opinions, and cultures play an important role in this issue—and this means a single object, a single meaning, a single image pictured in various different forms.

Every time a poet is about to write, every time they open their mouth to say something, they express their inner world and tell of their own feelings, thoughts, beliefs, and opinions, unless they are deliberately pursuing fantasies which contrast with their beliefs, opinions, thoughts, and point of view. As a matter of fact, it is possible to make the same remark about all other branches of art.

In this respect, we can say that the essence of poetry is based on one's inner voice and when performed in its proper tone, a poem purely reflects the poet's heart and feelings; therefore, it is revealed in different ways.

This act of revealing occurs sometimes as lines of words, sometimes as a few drops of wisdom, sometimes as an overflowing joy or a pitch-dark grief, sometimes as a bouquet of ardor, sometimes as heroics at full gallop, sometimes as homesickness, sometimes as the joy of reunion, or sometimes as multicolored pieces expressing a few of these notions together. No matter how, what essentially happens in poetry is the evaporation of metaphors, meanings and notions in wisps and their becoming "dew" within the poet's inner depths, and then their pouring into the bosom of pages like pure drops of rain.

True poetry is composed of metaphors and symbols which are born in the heart, rise like clouds, and assume a celestial form; verses formed otherwise are not poetry, but only artificial words, each of which contradicts the feelings inside. The utterances and words that have not been formed in a person's soul as the voice of conscience are all hollow, no matter how embellished they are or how dazzling they seem to be. A perfect poem owes its perfection to sounding the voice of the heart and the melodies of the conscience, as well as its ability to reflect the considerations, beliefs, opinions, and horizons of thought of the poet, but not due to its formal or mental aspects. The words of a great poet occur as an expression of the poet's inner feelings and senses, their love, enthusiasm, and interpretations, not as a linguistic effort. Reflecting the poet's own inner depths— overtly or covertly — is the touchstone for the sincerity of a poem and its being free from pretense. A true poet, whose considerations and imagery have their source in the inquiries and examinations of the conscience, always has a consistent style—with the exception of partial divergences at times—thus, voicing personal feelings, thoughts, and senses. Almost always the poet moves within the notes of a certain mode, both low and high, keeping within the same key. In fact, poetry is a word born of the appreciations, drafts, and preoccupations of the conscience, not a language; however, it constitutes an important ground for language to flourish. Sometimes, poetry can assume an equivocal, inexplicit form in terms of its wording; however, as a discourse it is always very clear and is timeless with respect to the richness of its content.

Poetry does not talk about humankind, the universe, and the Creator as religious studies, Sufism, and philosophy do. Just as in the case of dreams, poetry depicts meanings and metaphors as abstract images and motifs. Then its meaning is unfolded by interpreters in as many dimensions as their capacity allows them to appreciate its value. Whether or not a poet's conceptions, imaginings, and interpretations of a certain object accord with others' thoughts about the same thing, the frame of reference is the poet's own perception and the feelings that poets whisper to their tongue and pen are always related to this perception. The process of inner perception, evaluation, and expression that takes place in the poet also occurs in the person analyzing and interpreting the poem. The immensity and flexibility of the words can turn into a different voice and statement through the interpreter's overextending them owing to a difference of thought, opinion, and culture. The fact that it is possible to give opposing and contradictory interpretations of various people and ideas that are treated as if they were holy sources is a clear example of this. In this respect, we can say that just as poets express their inner world in poems they write, so an important point of reference for readers or interpreters are their own thoughts, opinions and culture. Though there may be exceptions, there is no doubt that this is the way it usually happens.

As a matter of fact, there is nothing very strange about this. Far from strange, it can even be considered desirable and beneficial given that the purity, innocence, and honor of one's words are in direct proportion to how well they voice the heart. Poetry is another name for a person's telling of the self, existence and what is beyond, and one's own perceptions. This is an important aspect of true poetry. Another aspect, which is no less important, is that these voices which spring from the heart and feelings should not tempt a person into carnal or material pitfalls, they should not pollute minds by describing falsehood, they should not try to lure readers or listeners by constructing fantasies or always pursuing weird things and exaggerating the subjects in question, they should not make every subject incomprehensible by trying to be obscure and ambiguous in an artificial attempt to seem thought-provoking, and so on. In a good poem, the wording should be exquisite, while love should reflect the longing for the essential source of all beauties. In addition, existence should be interpreted by seeing every object as a wonderful work of art and ascribing it to its True Owner. We can view all these features as the essentials of a poem's purity, innocence, and excellence.

A poem is not a poem in the true sense of the word if its relation to language consists of lies, exaggeration, and promoting the wrong, if its relation to imagination is transgression, obscenity, and pictures stimulating lust, and if its relation to consciousness and cognition is confined to beating the drum for deviant ideologies. Sets of words in such a dirty style are sometimes presented to us as poetry. But no matter what kind of an understanding is adopted, whether associated with positivism, which asserts that the truth can only be reached by trial and error, or rationalism, which asserts that everything can be explained and grasped by reason, whether the perspective of romanticism, which overemphasizes imagination and sensitivity, or an approach based on ardent naturalism, whether based on realism, which aims to describe everything as it is including its shortcomings, or a curiosity-raising approach such as surrealism, whether idealism, which asserts that there is nothing real but ideas, or cubism, which takes a geometric approach to everything instead of direct descriptions, or some other such current or perspective, that is not true poetry. True poetry is the perception of human feelings, the voice of the heart, open or hidden. It is the lyrics, composition, and melody of the relation between humankind, the universe and God, a shadow pinpointing each of the truths we can discern everywhere (from the earth to the stars), a photograph of the creation's projection cast in our feelings and thoughts and framed through words, a heartfelt tune of our loves and joys played on different strings, and it is a bouquet of our faith, hope, determination, beauty, love, reunion, and yearnings.

These are the characteristics of poetry with sound references and there is no exaggeration in them. The Qur'an describes poets who have not been able to find their true source and commit themselves to it: *As for poets, only the misguided follow them. Do you not see that they roam confusedly through all the valleys (of falsehoods, thoughts, and currents)*—the situation described may be that of poets who are stuck in the surface meaning of one of the different currents we have mentioned above; it is not of great importance that these currents had not appeared by the time this verse was revealed. The translation of the verse continues as follows: *And they say what they themselves do not do.* After that, the Qur'an emphasizes that such heedless poetry, which does not rest on an authentic basis, fires up carnal desires and fancies—or it is highly possible that they can do so. And then the Qur'an excepts the masters of poetry who base their words on an authentic reference, almost appreciating and praising them: *Except those who believe and do good, righteous deeds, and remember God much*... (Shuara 26:224–227).

Poetry in this sense of the word is such an atlas of expressions arranged from pearls of words and such a magical composition played on the most delicate strings of the heart that one who owns it can make everyone listen and influence them with it. When a poem like that finds the right tune and rings out, the most magnificent expressions stand saluting it in awe.

The foremost place in the dictionary of love belongs to poetry. The words that ascend the horizons of being heard by everyone on the wings of poetry can pass all boundaries and fly everywhere; they can speak to all nations and hand a flower to every soul. Up to now, such glorious floods of expression have overflowed from brilliant minds that over time they have discolored and turned into faint pictures or shallow streams; they have become the victims of familiarity so that no one pays attention to them anymore. As for a poem, which is true to its own origin and essentials, it always stays as fresh and vivid as a crown of words. And if this poem is also open to spirituality, then such words may ascend to be recited by heavenly beings.

Sometimes, even the most delightful samples of poetry might not display their beauties thoroughly. This is unfortunate for those works of excellence. However, such unfortunate states never last long; tomorrow, if not today, certain masters of words will surely hear them, and recognize and reveal their true value. As is the case today, poetry has often been treated as an object of no value and ignored by the masses. However, this indifference has never lasted long and the appreciative masters of words always crowned it in a becoming fashion, almost as a recompense for the reverence of which it had been deprived. In fact, poetry has always been like archives that peoples have continually used to serve their feelings, thoughts, national identities and cultures, and it has served as a factor uniting different historical periods. Those who had lost contact with their past for a certain period found and experienced the expression of their own selves in poetry, and they were able to see their history as a whole in it.

Poetry can be more eloquent than the most eloquent sermons, and it becomes a weapon more formidable than the sharpest of swords; whenever such a poem—which finds its correct tune and conveys the excitement of the heart—rings out, all the miserable, heaped drifts of words fly for shelter and bury themselves in ashamed silence. Whenever such a sword of poetry is drawn from its scabbard, all the false princes of words, who have set their thrones on a void, are thwarted and retreat into seclusion.

As for powerful poetry with sound content and meaning, the Messenger of God always sees it and indicates it as a source of wisdom. He had a rostrum set up in the Prophet's Mosque for Hassan ibn Thabit to recite poems; then he prayed for the poet, saying, "My God, support him with the Holy Spirit." This can be seen as emphasizing the value of struggling with the diamond sword of poetry against the crude heathen mentality.

So far as a poem retains its own color, we cannot find a beauty which is as fresh, as vivid or as ageless. Though poetry does not have a color of its own, it is a reality that it carries some tints from every color. When letters and words become students in the school of poetry, when they become recruits in the ranks of poetry, words reach all levels of knowledge and they conquer all strongholds.

In fact, existence is arranged like a poem written into the framework of the laws of creation. As for poetry, which has become a strong voice and word through its own dynamics, it is another way of voicing the same poem of existence in a variety of forms by different strings of speech. In this respect, we can consider poets to be the nightingales of existence and the beyond. As stated in the verse: *We have not taught him (the Messenger) poetry; further, it is not seemly for him.* (Yasin 36:69), God's Messenger is not a conveyor of feelings, emotions, and perceptions but of pure divine truths. Neither is he a poet, nor is the Qur'an poetry. However, the Prophet is a prince of exposition and the most glorious master of all people of words, while the Qur'an is one of the brightest and richest sources of poets who are "inspired." The prophets explain the essence of the relation between humankind, the universe, and the Creator in a way understandable to everyone. They guide people on how to serve God Almighty, guidance that brings happiness in both worlds. As for poets, they express these truths or other subordinate matters in a new style in accord with their own perceptions, comprehension, horizons, characters, and temperaments in the language of their hearts, feelings and emotions.

True poetry is a fruit flourishing like a heavenly flower on the branches of inspiration such that similar fruits replace it depending on the thoughts and intentions of those who will pick the fruit. Then this wondrous crop is renewed unceasingly. So much so that the hands which reach to the tree of poetry find something to pluck every time; however, all that is plucked retains its uniqueness. Neither the senses and feelings, nor the new blossoms repeat themselves because feelings, thoughts, intentions, perspectives, and cultures are what bring the fruit its real hue, taste, and accent. Indeed, though poetry is a thought heated in the crucible of consciousness and cognition and a melody sounded through the instrument of language, what gains true depth and genuine hue are the horizons of the poet's belief, opinion, culture, and thought. If the words which have found their true state by boiling in such a crucible rise up with belief, opinion, and culture, then they become transcendent and attain depth as lofty as in the heavenly beings' exchange of words. They become a river of wisdom which has wondrous results everywhere it passes. When the poem catches the fine point to be expressed and speaks for it, it echoes within the souls of men and women of letters like the trumpet Sur blown by the Archangel Israfil. In our time when faint words devoid of purpose, spirit, and background blacken our horizons like a curtain black as pitch, we obviously thirst for true poetry. Nevertheless, neither am I capable of, nor is the length of a short essay enough for a true expression of this thirst.

WOMAN: A SOURCE OF MERCY

Woman was created a magnificent example of affection with respect to her inner faculties; affection is a part of her temperament and nature by creation. A woman of this pure nature—if not spoiled by mistaken interference—always thinks of affection, speaks of affection, sits and stands in affection, watches those around her in affection throughout her life, and offers glassfuls of affections to everybody. At the same time she suffers for them from within, due to her refinement and sincerity. She cares for everybody—her parents, siblings, friends, and all relatives—and, when the time comes, for her spouse and children. As she shares pleasure, delight, and joy, she blooms like a rose with sweet smiles for those around her. Upon seeing their grief and sorrow, she grows pale, withers, and groans with pain.

She wants to see beautiful things, and to be surrounded by beauty. However, she sometimes finds what she expects and sometimes does not. Sometimes the wind keeps blowing so harshly around her and shakes everything close to her heart. Then her heart cannot settle wherever she goes, she is constantly on pins and needles, and she breathes through tears from within. And at other times the beauties in her range of vision make her as joyful as a child and she fills those around her with cheer.

A woman who has found her match with respect to depth of soul and who has quenched her thirst with her children is no different than the women of Paradise, and the home structured around such a person is no different than the gardens of Paradise. And it is no wonder that her children, who grow up savoring affection in the shelter of this paradise, will be no different than heavenly beings. Indeed those who are fortunate enough to be raised in such an atmosphere of affection will live in a state of otherworldly joy as if they have been exalted to the heavens, inspiring high spirits all around through their smiles.

In such a home, even if they seem separate in the body, the soul that governs everybody and everything is one. And this soul, which always wells up from the woman and embraces the entire home, makes its presence felt like a spell or a spirit, and virtually guides them in certain directions. A blessed woman who has not restricted the potential of her heart and is open to spirituality is like the North Star in the family solar system; she retains her position and spins around herself, and all the other members of the family shape their stances around her, and march towards their aims in devotion to her. In fact, everybody else's relation with the home is temporary, limited and relative. But a woman, whether she has other jobs or not, always stands up straight in the heart of her home and nourishes our feelings with affection, mercy, and love.

A woman who is totally oriented towards eternity in her thoughts and feelings, inspires our spirits with emotions that no other master or teacher can make us feel; she adorns our hearts with the most splendid inscription of the most wonderful meanings never to fade in time or be erased by anybody. Then, with the spiritual background she provides us, she presents to us priceless potential riches for our later life. In the presence of this perfect woman (*insan al-kamila*), we constantly sense the mercy, affection, and poetry of the worlds beyond pouring into our souls, and we always breathe with the joy of otherworldliness deep inside.

To us, woman, particularly as a mother, is as deep as the heavens and is a blend of feelings and affections filling her heart like the numerous stars of the skies. She is always content with her share, whether it is bitter or sweet, at peace with her joys and sorrows, intimate with joy and concern, and closed to grudge and hatred. She, in a constant effort to revive and restore, is the purest core of humanity's vicegerency of God, and the essence of human subtlety. Especially, a fortunate woman who has opened the doors of her heart to eternity through her belief and notion of infinity, holds such a brilliant position beyond imagination, such a magical point—which can be described as the unified realm of the physical and spiritual or body and soul—that the greatest titles or posts we could give her would look like flickering candles before her real merits, which shine like suns; such titles, which are based on superficial and unfair assumptions about her place, position, and qualities, overshadow her genuine worth.

Woman, in our world of thought and atlas of values is the most significant color of the phenomenon of creation, the most fruitful and magical component of humanity, a faultless projection of the beauties of paradise in homes, and the most reliable blessing for humanity's existence and continuity. Prior to her creation, Prophet Adam was alone, the eco-system was devoid of spirit, man was doomed to extinction; the home was merely a den, no different than a tree hollow, and man's existence was confined to his own lifetime. With her, a second pole was formed, and the two poles became connected. Existence became enlivened with a new and different voice and vision; creation entered into the phase of completion, and the lone human turned into a species and became one of the most important elements of the universe. Thanks to her coming her spouse earned merits beyond all other values.

Although women, physiologically and psychologically, have a different nature and characteristics from men, that does not denote any superiority of man over woman or vice versa. We can think of woman and man as Nitrogen and Oxygen in the air; they are both vital in terms of their special roles and functions, and need one another to the same degree. Making comparisons between men and women is as absurd as contrasting the substances in the air, saying things like, "Nitrogen is more valuable," or, "Oxygen is more beneficial." In fact, man and woman are identical in terms of their creation and their mission in the world, and are like two different faces of the whole in mutual need of one another.

Indeed, God has created woman as partner to man, and not as anything else. Adam could not be without Eve, and Eve could not be without Adam. This very first couple, were entrusted with the important duty of being mirror and interpreter, both in the name of their Creator and on the part of the creation. They were like two bodies and a single soul and represented two different faces of one truth. In time, rough understandings and crude thinking have upset this balance; with that, both the harmony of the family and the social order were upset too.

As a matter of fact, as Ibn Farid put it, the beauty of woman and that of man was each a glimmer of the beauty of the Creator, the Most Beautiful. These two marvels of creation accepted each other as they were and supported one another, hand in hand, shoulder to shoulder. This raised them to another level of beauty higher than the one they were already at. Approaches and ways outside the framework of their creation make them ugly and rough. Beauty and elegance are most meaningful with spiritual (as opposed to material) qualities, and a woman is regarded as a multi-dimensional mirror of the beauty of the manifestation of the divine. This potential might turn into a means of mischief if she dims herself with the darkest hues of human nature and narrows down her scope of duty of being a mirror by binding everything to physicality.

As long as woman is conscious of her inner depth and remains within the limits of her nature, she becomes such a bright mirror reflecting the beauties of the essence of the creation that those who look at her from a decent perspective and perceive her correctly free themselves from the darkness of physicality at once. And they ascend to the horizons of enjoyment of the divine beauties and sing in their hearts

> *Sun of the beauty of the pretty faces set down in the end;*
> *I am the lover of the Everlasting Beauty and say, "I love not those*
> *that set."*[9]

---

[9] A part of the verse (6:76) from the Qur'an, in which the story of Prophet Abraham is narrated: "I love not those that set."

THE HORIZON OF THE HEART AND SPIRIT

When the heart is mentioned, the first thing that comes to our mind is the organ resembling a pine cone in the left part of the chest, just under the left breast, which has both nerves and muscles, atriums and ventricles, which acts autonomously and is the root and center of veins and arteries, and which is also related to respiration and the movements of the lungs. However, what we mean here by the word "heart" is the spiritual or divine faculty, which is one of the four basic elements of the conscience, and the center of our world of feelings, thoughts, consciousness, sensing, cognition, and spirituality. It is the heart in this sense which is the essence of the truth of being human.

The faculty to which we refer with the word heart is a stairway leading to human perfection, a projection of the realms beyond in the corporeal world, the largest door within the human body open to spirituality, the sole laboratory where our selfhood is formed, and the most important criterion of telling right from wrong. Our relation with our spirit, making use of our minds in a positive way, and studying and analyzing our human inclinations are all reliant on this center. So it is this heart which becomes over time the sight and hearing of our spirit; in accordance with the "point of reliance and point of seeking help" (*nokta-i istinat, nokta-i istimdat*), which are deeper dimensions of the heart, our sensations and perceptions become the heart's sight, our mind becomes its analyzer, and our willpower its director and administrator.[10]

---

10 See *Wijdan* (Conscience) in Gülen, *Key Concepts in the Practice of Sufism Vol. 3* for more discussion on the four components of conscience and how they are related: the heart, the willpower, the mind, and the power of perceptiveness.

The source of provision or nutrition for this spiritual heart is faith, and its way to contentment is the continuous remembrance of God. As the Qur'an states: *Be aware that it is in the remembrance of, and whole-hearted devotion to God, that hearts find rest and contentment* (Ra'd 13: 28). Only in this way do the pains in the soul abate, and stresses and depressions are overcome. And then the breezes of contentment start to blow in our world of feelings. This is because everything started with God. He is the Primary Source such that all causes, which seem to extend as if in unending cycles or links, finally end in Him. All desires, wishes, and expectations conclude in Him in the end. He is the First, before Whom there was nothing and with Whom there is nothing like the second; He is the final Refuge, after Whom there is nothing. Neither in the corporeal world nor in our inner world and faculty of conscience can we talk about anything beyond Him. He is the ultimate beyond, with nothing further beyond. When He is remembered in full recognition, human thought reaches its ultimate horizons, intellect and logic reach the level of bewilderment and amazement,[11] and the spirit reaches the farthest point which mortal beings can possibly reach. This is the point where all expectations may come true, where all worldly anxieties turn out to be groundless, where causes topple over one by one and everything is dyed in Divine Oneness.

While until this point everything humankind turns toward— blessings and gratitude, joys and relief, finding and contentment— takes place with the aim of reaching for the better, everything suddenly finishes on reaching this very point. After having reached Him, all desires and wishes end, all the excitements of spiritual journeying instantly cease and feelings and thoughts become mercy, like moisture condensing into dew. Then all the wishes to ascend within the domain of causality come to an end, and the need to seek an authority vanishes from minds. And one feels joy as if they were strolling up the long path they had been following. From

---

11 For an explanation of "amazement" (*hayra*) in the Sufi sense, see *Dahsha* and *Hayra* in Gülen, *Key Concepts in the Practice of Sufism*, Volume I.

then on, however, the journey continues with breezes of tranquility, which blow beyond all the measures of quantity and quality in different wavelengths of Divine manifestations and are combined with uninterrupted love and joyful zeal and feelings of reunion.[12]

This spiritual heart within the human essence has a mysterious relation with the physical heart, similar to that between the body and soul. However, it has not so far been possible to say anything definite about the nature of these two relations. We acknowledge in principle that almost all of what has been said about this topic up to today can refer to any aspect of the truth; however this subject is not essential to our discussion here.

The spirit's relation to the "spiritual life" and "spirituality" is very obvious.[13] The Qur'an says, *"the spirit is of my Lord's command"* (al-Isra 17:85). This statement is extremely meaningful in terms of emphasizing the fact that the reality of the spirit is something only the Creator can know; nobody but God can know the truth of the spirit.

The spirit is a law with external existence, a law with consciousness from the Realm of Divine Commands and the Divine Attribute of Will, just like the laws of creation, which are fixed realities with continuous existence. Both the spirit and the laws operating in the universe are of the same nature, and they come from the Realm of Divine Commands. They are identical with respect to their source and their being perpetual. Said Nursi explains the spirit as follows: "If the Divine Power clothed the laws operating in the universe with external, perceptible bodies, they would become spirits. On the other hand, if God stripped consciousness from spirits, they would become laws, like the different laws operating in the universe."[14] This pithy explanation of the truth of the spirit, to which the Qur'an alludes in a few words, is strong enough to put an end to all the metaphysical arguments about its essence and reality. As a matter of fact,

---

12 Ibid. *Asq* and *Ishtiyaq*.

13 These two epistemological concepts need further analysis independently studied under the discipline of Sufism.

14 From "Seeds of Truth" in the Damascus Sermon of Said Nursi, No. 19.

every Divine act is instantly realized without requiring the existence or intermediary function of any physical cause, condition, means, or material. When He wills to create something, He just gives the command "Be!" and it is. This command is sufficient for anything to come into external, perceptible existence. In other words, it is sufficient for something to be with a certain nature that God Almighty wills it to be. Even though the continual instances of coming into existence like this seem to the mind like ordinary happenings, it is impossible for them to be accounted for without attributing them to the real Giver of commands.

When we consider spirit, we sometimes refer to the Supreme Spirit (*Ruh al-A'zam*), which is a breath of God Almighty and denotes the most perfect level of spiritual existence. We do so because it is from God, and it is this spirit which is nearest to Him, and inherent in it are the secrets belonging to the Realm of Transcendental Manifestations of Divinity. Also, humankind's being God's vicegerent on earth is because of their having such a spirit. This spirit within human beings is both a gift from a realm having nothing to do with materiality to the corporeal realm and like a tongue, a translator, of metaphysical considerations. First of all, this essence, which we call the spirit, is a manifestation from both the Realms of Divine Knowledge and Existence; it is a conscious law from the Realm of Divine Commands because of its relation to the Divine Essence, and is luminous and transparent due to its perfect capacity to learn and know its Creator. If one wishes to be open to Divine secrets—given that everybody is created with the necessary potential to realize this—this will be possible only through the heart and spirit. As the secrets related to the truth of Divinity can be viewed only from the horizon of the heart through the eye of the spirit, so nearness to God beyond intellect, logic, and reasoning, and beyond all causes can be realized only by means of the spirit and the rules of the heart.

The spirit is an observer and the heart is its special observatory; the spirit is an athlete on the path to God and the heart is its most vital source of energy; the spirit is a traveler and the heart is a guide leading it to its destination; we can even say that the heart is a mysterious meeting place of the soul with its true Beloved beyond any measures or modalities of quantity and quality. For this reason, if one is to turn toward eternity, they should first of all turn toward the door of heart, they should keep telling stories of the heart, mingle with people of heart, and make their spirit wear feathers from the wings of the heart, so that they may not be hindered by the obstacles of the physical world. On the way to eternity, the heart is a person's hand or wing; it is a dynamo taking its energy from the realms beyond. Those who have the support of the power of the heart and set about the journey toward the heavens under its guidance do not need any other means whatsoever. They keep up their journeying abreast with spirit beings. These souls who run to he nearness of the Divine Throne without tiring are like riders of the heart who have largely freed themselves from carnal concerns. The sounds of angels' wings are heard all the time in the very realms where they flap their wings.

With its intermediary existence between this world and the next, the inner and outer dimensions of existence, the physical and metaphysical worlds, the heart, which has been created at the intersection point of spiritual and material realms and bears the seal of the Creator, is like a Universal Human among human beings. It has a very extensive area of contact. With such extensiveness, it is that which is enveloped at the same time as it is that which envelops, and something which encompasses while it is encompassed. While inside the body, the heart is the true source of its life; it is the body's guide on the path to eternity even though it seems to be bound to physicality. The spirit is open to illuminations due to the light of the heart, and it is attractive owing to its essential attractiveness.

Within human nature, the physical form and life are like secondary elements in the tow of the heart's essence. In fact, the value held by both the appearance and life completely derives from the heart. The intellect has always woven its most lasting works in the atmosphere of the heart. When the inspirations of the heart surround the mind from all sides, all the false lights related to logic and reasoning disappear; only and nothing but the candle of the heart, whose wax and wick have their source in the realms beyond, keeps shining brightly.

Pure clear waters keep flowing in the fountain of the heart, which is supplied from infinity. Around the lantern-glass of the heart, whose light and color comes from the realms beyond, spirit beings keep circling like butterflies all the time. Those who manage to reach such a fountain of life can be considered to have laid their prayer mat on the same green sward as Khadr.[15] And those who have this lantern-glass in their pupils do not wish to part from that source of light again. The raising of the veil on the face of the heart and the awakening of the heart's eye to eternity depends completely on time and active patience. Since the eyes of the hearts of those who make good use of time and practice this patience will certainly open, tomorrow if not today, it should not be doubted that their tongues will become waterfalls of proclamation in time. When the time comes and their hearts are enlightened with the lights of the horizons they have reached, and when their tongue is unbound, they perform such lovely melodies that they charm everyone.

The heart is a horizon that is so open to divine secrets that the commotion of angels and the wing claps of spirit beings are heard a mere two steps away. For those who reach such a station of secrets, the Sidra[16] and the Ka'ba virtually become an integrated whole. The Prophet's Rawda[17] becomes a cover of the Paradise of Firdaws.[18]

---

15 Khadr (Khidr): A blessed person who represents eternal enlivening or the gaining of eternity through elixir. (Tr.)

16 Sidratul Muntaha, or the Lote Tree of the Farthest Length, is the name of the spiritual station the Prophet reached during the night of Ascension and it denotes the ultimate proximity to God.

17 The Garden of the Prophet, or Rawda, is the area between his blessed tomb and pulpit where he used to deliver his sermons. It is reported that the Prophet once said, "Between my home and pulpit lies a garden of Paradise."

18 Highest abode in Paradise. The Prophet said, "Ask God for the Firdaws, for it is the highest abode in Paradise."

The divine name Al-Awwal[19] assumes the color of Al-Akhir[20]... Al-Zahir[21] is dyed in the color of Al-Batin[22]... one's feelings are struck with the utmost astonishment,[23] the spirit feels amazement... speech takes a step back... the heart sets about speaking through the tongue of the soul. And everything is charmed with the charm of infinity.

The speaking of heart-oriented people is without letters and words; they always speak through their spirits. As Rumi also expressed it, they converse with one another without tongues or lips... . They keep smiling at one another from the color of their hearts, which is reflected in their faces like roses. Among these souls who have completely immersed themselves in the dye of the heart, the idea of "you" or "I" completely disappears and what remains behind is a relative "us," which depends on "Him." In this respect, they never compete with one another, do not try to extinguish the light of the other, and they do not seek priority and say, "my candle" or "my torch." As a matter of fact, light does not challenge another light, spring does not fight against greenery, the sea does not dry a drop. One shining thing only makes another shine more, the rays of one light come to the aid of another, the spring lives intermingled with greenery, the sea paves the way to immortality for the drop.... Every single thing and whispers to us poems of being "us."

As far as a person depends on his own person, he cannot be saved from being an atom, a drop, and even a nothing. On the other hand, when people shatter the glass of the ego and merge with others in the immensity of their heart and attain a different nature out of their own narrow world, they immediately become a sun, an ocean, and a universe. Like raindrops which unite and become a waterfall, they virtually become rivers and take the path to infinity, and they rise to a surpassing value. And if they fail to attain such a

---

19 The First, Whom there is none that precedes.

20 The Last, Who eternally exists while all other beings are perishable.

21 The All-Outward, Who encompasses the whole of existence from outside, and there is none that encompasses Him.

22 The All-Inward, Who encompasses the whole existence from within in His knowledge.

23 see *Dahsha* and *Hayra* in Gülen, *Key Concepts in the Practice of Sufism*, Volume I.

value, they remain within worldly and material values whose worth only lasts until the grave. When they die one day, everything ends, and they just drift away like dried leaves in fall. As for the roses, the flowers of the heart's garden, they remain ever fresh and never fade. Here are a few beautiful words expressing the suffering of a soul who has attached everything to worldliness:

> *Some of them hurt the conscience, and some the body;*
> *Whatever I did for pleasure, I regretted.*

Namık Kemal

And listen to these hopeful words, all of which are the voice of the heart:

> *In this world all the flow'rs wither,*
> *The sweet songs of the birds are brief;*
> *I dream of summers that will last*
> *Always!*
> *...*
> *In this world ev'ry man is mourning*
> *His lost friendship or his lost love;*
> *I dream of fond lovers abiding*
> *Always!*

Sully Prudhomme

And now let us listen to these prayer-like words which relate everything to the delight of an immense appreciation of the divine:

> *...I am mortal, but I do not want the mortal.*
> *I am impotent, so I do not desire the impotent.*
> *I surrendered my spirit to the All-Merciful One,*
> *so I desire none else.*
> *I want only One Who will remain my friend forever.*
> *I am but an insignificant particle,*
> *but I desire an everlasting sun.*
> *I am nothing in essence,*
> *but I wish for the whole of creation.*

Said Nursi (Seventeenth Word)

Undesirable things are those that will leave us after two steps. And what is truly desirable is the Beloved One, Who is always beheld on the horizons of the heart. Those who ascend to the peaks of the heart and behold[24] Him through the eye of the soul can be considered to have found everything and to be saved. As for those who live unaware of such a point of observation, they eternally moan with longing and grief. And the way to ascend such a citadel depends on ridding oneself of the wall of biological life and turning toward the life levels of the heart and spirit. The fastest means to do this, which helps a rapid ascent, is to be constantly open to the truths of faith, divine oneness, and knowledge of God.

---

24 What is translated here as "behold" (*tamasha*) denotes an awareness of God, rather than a literal seeing, which is impossible in the corporeal world. (Ed.)

AN EXTENSIVE WISH IN THE VIEW OF
HISTORICAL RECURRENCES

Since the creation of humankind, day followed night, and light was accompanied by dark. Just like the alternation of light and dark over the Earth, bright days were followed by days of pitch dark, and relief-laden eras were replaced by periods of crisis. From time to time, almost every corner was obscured by the darkness of unbelief and conflict. Roads were left without illumination. Humanity was defeated by darkness. Some unfettered people with vain ideas crowded the scene, spreading their inauspicious muttering throughout the world. At times, the collective conscience held its breath in the face of the noise they made, entering into a contemplative silence. Then, the word fell into disrepute. Slaves acquired the seal of authority. Masses became toys of demagogy. They were manipulated to silence or action at will. Unsuitable persons were declared stars while many talented persons were barred from stardom. False pretensions and dialectical philosophy blocked logic and reasoning. Evil thoughts replaced decent ideas. The institutions from which society expected mercy and compassion were occupied by crude souls obsessed with hatred and animosity. Using these institutions, they sowed seeds of mischief among people, making them enemies of each other. Horrendous damage was done to religious thought; parameters were undermined and everything turned into chaos. Cups of sweet drink were replaced with goblets of poison, dishes of honey and cream with pots of filth, and light with darkness.

In these dreadful and ominous eras, minds became so confused that people could not help but feel agitated, even when they extended a hand to the most decent and noblest of things. Without trust, we referred to each other as "wild," "animal," "savage," and "barbarian." The faithful and conscientious people, if they were any, were humiliated and rendered speechless. The slaves of darkness became ferocious while the souls who longed for light waited for a helping hand to appear on the horizon of miraculous blessings; they yearned for sunrises; they daydreamed of times that would emerge from mercy. When lips would twitch with the tiniest of smiles out of these considerations they were swept away by subsequent storms of worry; temporary moments of happiness were effectively replaced with years of sorrow.

In line with the notion "history repeats itself," the foregoing account applies to our time as well. All of a sudden, clear and sunny horizons are covered with mist and smoke, our view is blocked and our hearts shudder with gloom. Days of joy are dim. Darkness shades our thoughts; our wills are cracked, and our hopes are demolished. At times, one feels as if the sun will never rise again and that daylight will never appear. Unguided souls are shivering with internal desperation and resultant curses.

As for us, as always, we are sure that the latest chaos boiling with filth will soon be terminated, and felicitous days will come in which divine destiny will clear roads for our society. As a matter of fact, stories of people of heart are already being related everywhere. Everywhere, pure souls are breathless with the desire to find the Paradise they have lost. Hundreds or thousands of people are meditating upon such considerations, contemplating the purpose of creation and the causes of nature. Yet, we are passing through a rather foggy period of time with respect to our spiritual lives. Moreover, a chilling wind blows for a while, filling the air with the vibration of sorrow. Even the places that overflow with ultimate joy are, from time to time, suffused with worry and despair. Nevertheless, we all know well that worry and despair can no longer stand firm. And when the horizons are bright to help us distinguish good from evil, all the hardships endured on the road will be immediately mitigated. Distances will readily submit to endeavors and efforts. Hills will turn into valleys, and valleys will become smoother; and then, ideals will be intertwined with the journey, and no trace of hardship will be felt in the face of the glamour of the horizons of the goal.

Nowadays, hands are reaching out, though feebly, to the rope of the heart, and the breaths of the soul are heard everywhere. Reason and heart go hand in hand. Thought is embracing inspiration with its dazzling depths. Logic is subordinated to divine revelation. Science guides us to faith; knowledge is led by intuitive knowledge; laboratories raise apprentices to the prayer hall; wills are lively and resolute with the help of the water of life that is offered by faith; eyes wander on the same horizons with insight; contradicting physics, metaphysical springs emerge everywhere. It seems obvious that snow or ice, however cold they are, cannot survive long in the face of the heat kindled in the sources. Blizzards, however strong they are, will fail to extinguish the torches protected by the lanterns of the natural tendencies of human nature—as long as it is permitted by God. Although, at times, most of us turn crimson red, shivering with various worries or making a fuss over strong winds, it is obvious that we send our warmest smiles to our surroundings like roses bursting from their buds, effervescing like nightingales flitting from one branch to another. We cannot deny the fact that our hearts leap with hope and expectation for the sounds of "waterfalls of life" to reach us, for "the white hand"[25] to hover over our heads. The already awakened souls ponder these considerations with confidence; it is as if they have reached the borders of their hearts, and are full of joy with the enthusiasm of having sensed the odors of Paradise, however slight the trickle of its scent may be.

---

[25] The miraculous hand of Prophet Moses.

Yes, those capable of filtering current events through their hearts and souls can feel the coming of spring, which brings a shining sun and all the shades of green under foot. Waterfalls of assistance and effort gurgle in the bed of divine blessings, heading toward the sea free from all obstacles; they pass over or flow around any obstruction they meet and they try to represent the mission endowed by divine destiny in detail with the beautiful geometric lines they leave behind. As they walk, the roads hail them; seemingly insurmountable obstacles are flattened and nullified, as if they are prostrating themselves before these holy ones.

As a matter of fact, this state is always the case for the matured souls: at all times, they send fragrance to their surroundings like censers. Burning like sticks of incense, they convey the joy of burning to everybody through their moans. When necessary, they roar like lions, displaying their characters. When necessary, they sing like nightingales, filling souls with joy and relief. Their foreheads have been impressed with the seal of being both dear and humble; they are neither oppressed nor are they tyrants. It is a spectacular sight when they show their modesty before their Lord, acting humbly to the highest extent. In short, they are the heroes who have managed to merge lion-like manners with dove-like customs in the same vessel, and those who are gifted in getting to know their inner depths always want to be with them.

How I wish my body would always shiver like swaying trees before my Lord in a state of openness to this delicacy, knocking on His door with a yearning for acceptance! How I wish I could occupy myself with my own faults instead of concentrating on the errors I observe here and there, and ignore their mistakes! How I wish I could detect my own defects and failures at each beat of my pulsing heart! It is my sincere wish that the values to be weighed on the scale of life be the products of conscientious reckoning that have been filtered through my internal contemplations. It is my sincere wish that my balance sheet is always high on the asset side, and that all credit is attributed to Him for the achievements I have been blessed with—I continuously long to completely forget comfort and languor, to seek the peace of the heart in toil, and to become calm with hardship. I yearn to moan like Job and to cry like David for my faults and for my erroneous manners, no matter how small—I long to devote myself to the peace and security of humankind as long as I live. I have a desire to have so vast a love that it will embrace everybody with warmth and non-discrimination and I wish to be forgetful of rage, hate, and animosity.

Now, let us devote ourselves to the deep illumination of humankind; let us melt like candles in our endeavors so as to illuminate our remote or close environment in preference to our selfish desires. Wherever we go, let us be the voice and translator of the truth with a spirit of real devotion, telling of Him and communicating His message. Let us be so respectful in our relations with God and so sincere in submission to Him that we make celestial angels envy our manners and make spiritual beings feel obliged to retreat a few steps in the face of the meanings that overflow from our selves. Let us wrap our selves in the color of the dawns that follow the nights on which the most sincere prayers are offered to God and assume the role assigned to us at the time of creation; let us conduct ourselves well. Let us put an end to our comfort without fearing hardships and run so swiftly that birds watch us in awe; let us cry out the truth with such sincerity that wild creatures fearfully seek refuge in their lairs. When we feel like a lion, let us not instill fear in people; let us instead attempt to cast off the shackles on our will. When we feel like fire, let us not ignite new fires, but illuminate the people around us by lighting candles. When we turn into a flood, let us flow gently toward gardens and orchards to give them life. When we blow like winds, let us carry seeds for propagation; let us bring drops of moisture together to teach the clouds how to become rain as a divine mercy.

Indeed, we must show earnest respect to those esteemed by God. God treats and views people differently. He may place a person at the forefront to serve as an altar in glorifying Him. He may whisper the enigma of existence into their soul, crowning them with a special caliphate. By taking this person to new horizons through faith and intuitive knowledge, He enables them to feel the truth of His presence. He prepares eternal happiness for such people in the Hereafter. He opens doorways to the Paradise in their heart; He makes this dungeon-like world a waiting room for the coming Paradise. He honors those who manage all their actions based on insight in this world by allowing them to watch His beauty in the Hereafter. He brings thousands of aspects to one-dimensional living. In their magical worlds, He transforms seas into the rose-covered slopes of Paradise, and ever-boiling hells into babbling springs of life. He creates new worlds with incredible wonders for them every day.

Certainly, those who live in this world as if blind, deaf, and dead will not even get a glimpse of the above. Those who act unwarily, even taking lightly these grave conditions today will be likely to continually wail in penitence in future. Then, let us be vigilant today so that we will not be troubled for rest and sleep tomorrow. Let us weep abundantly today so that we will not cry from regret tomorrow. Let us concentrate at all times on the horizon to which we are heading, so as not to be distracted by the attractive things on the side of the road. If we fail to regard this world as a marketplace where trade is carried out for gains to be taken onto the Hereafter and do not manage our life accordingly, if we lead our life in line with the whims of carnal desires, then we should not be surprised when one day somebody puts a packsaddle on us and mounts us. This is indeed the kind of treatment that the narrow-minded, the feckless, and conceited people will receive. The value of humankind is directly proportional to the degree of their connection with God and the continuation of their sincere relations with Him. A human-shaped body contaminated with carnal desires and alienated from Him will have less value than mud, even if decorated with gold, silver, and satin.

Then, come and liberate yourself from bodily worries and carnal troubles! Turn toward Him with your whole existence and fix your gaze on Him, for in this way these initial gifts will increase greatly in value! Never forget that His favor turns a drop of water into a sea, a particle into a sun, and transforms your impotence and poverty into your greatest strength. On the other hand, if you rely on your own power, you will blunder—like trying to heat great cauldrons with a single spark, you will lay yourself open to ridicule. Know the limits of your power and resources, and make your plans accordingly. If you ignore this important point and set on building facts on fancies, whatever you do will come tumbling down, crushing your faith and hopes. Assess yourself frequently through internal self-criticism and contemplation, specify your position well according to your capabilities and resources, and be aware of the relation between your potential and the effort you have exerted. Avoid becoming "a carrier of divine gifts with no fidelity," that is, try not to be regarded as a spoiled person who has become arrogant because of the patronage of other people.

Rely on divine grace to the highest degree, but never fail to fulfill whatever free will requires of you. Do not expect secondary winds to carry you to your target; consider the fact that those who have been taken to higher levels by today's winds may one day be thrown into the deepest pits by tomorrow's storms; try to live in line with realities.

Know that religion is a road leading to divine proximity, and sincerely hold fast to a life led by religion. Seek shelter in the secure harbor of faith, and submit to the Creator! Never falter in reliance on Him and keep your manners always decent before Him; endeavor to be a modest believer without any vanity or ostentation! Saturated hearts are silent like boxes fully loaded with ore. Empty souls make a great deal of noise just like children's money boxes that contain a few fake pearls. Always remember that your heart is monitored by God many times every instant, and therefore keep your heart clean and immaculate at all times, and you will head toward that eternal altar! Until now, whoever has headed toward that altar has never lost while whoever sought faithfulness from other places has never won. Rather, those who sought shelter at that gate have remained lively and have been honored with eternity, saved from the disgrace of being slaves of other entities. When one finds Him and faces Him, when one reveals one's deepest feeling in His presence, one glorifies and exalts Him. To remain silent is to contemplate in meditation and self-criticism. Those who manage to be in His presence and proximity always feel the water of life, even if they are in a desert; those who rely on Him in all their acts always reap roses, even if they have sown thorn bushes. Even under hell-like conditions, they are always calm and at peace. And the following is their motto:

> *Servants of God cannot be slaves to another slave,*
> *Never will true servants be stranded.*
> *Their souls are filled with joy in reunion,*
> *Never will they be deceived, even if everybody else is*

Perhaps, we will find an opportunity to deal with this issue one day.

IMPLICATIONS OF THE BIRTH
OF THE PROPHET

He is the one who has raised the veil on the face of creation and unearthed the secrets ingrained in the spirit of things. By removing the disruption in between he recoupled the earth with the heavens. He made the mind and the heart meet within the frame of the soundest essentials, thus liberating the power of reasoning to metaphysical immensities. He is the one who has unraveled the truth behind all things, living or non-living, and he established his interpretations on universal rules much earlier than everyone else and at a level that surpassed that of the greatest scientists. He is the one who said the most essential words about the universe, who probed things and events with his words and drew aside the veil of secrets in order for us to behold that which is beyond everything. It was he who exalted human thought to the point of intersection between body and soul and who turned this corporeal world into a corridor to the heavens, shattering obsolete understandings. He is the Prophet Muhammad, the final Messenger of God, peace be upon him.

In this world, in which we used to live heedlessly, we have learned about our Creator through the Prophet. We have felt and become aware of the blessings that shower down on us thanks to the illumination he provided for our vision. We have learned from him once again feelings of gratitude for blessings, the notion of perfect goodness (*ihsan*) and praising God. Thanks to the messages he brought to us, we are able to comprehend the relationship between the Creator and the created, the relationship between the worshipper and the worshipped in a way that is fitting to the greatness of the Creator and becoming to our servanthood.

Before he set foot in this world—his foot is our crown—light and darkness were intermingled, the ugly and beautiful went side by side, roses were pierced by thorns, sugar remained hidden in the cane, the earth was dark to spite the sky, the sky was a terrible and chilling void, the metaphysical was confined to the narrow considerations of physicality, the spiritual was overshadowed by the corporeal, the spirit was a dry and empty phrase, and the heart was obscured by the flesh. It was thanks to the light that he poured on our vision that all the former world and worn-out thoughts fell, one by one... darkness was overpowered by light. And once more, the soul and spirituality took the reins. It was thanks to the interpretations he made about humankind, existence, and God that the universe became a comprehensive and legible book of the Divine. From one end to the other, this huge universe became an exhibition of Divine art. Natural phenomena became nightingales that related tales of the Creator, calling to God, and proclaiming the praises of God's ability to create perfectly out of nothing.

Feelings were in darkness until the eyes of humanity awakened to his light; thoughts were inconsistent and hearts were brought down by loneliness. There was neither joy without grief, nor was there a sign of pleasure without pain. There was not one single drop from the realms beyond, so the slopes of the heart were devoid of spring or greenery. By his honoring this world, the spell of the drought that prevailed everywhere was broken. The eyes in the heavens filled with tears, and hearts assumed the color of the slopes of Paradise. And then the suffering of the hearts, which had dried and cracked from the drought, came to an end. And the fountain of light appeared on the horizons of the souls that had been writhing in agony in the claws of death.

Until the moment he honored this derelict world, lies and truth were intermingled, goodness and sins were companions, the notion of virtue was an obscure concept, and dishonesty was rife in the market of passing desires and fancies. The condition of all of humanity was dreadful because of the life they led, which was in complete contradiction to the true purpose of their creation; they had the stamp of rebellion on their foreheads and delirium in their souls. Almost everyone was anxiously watching out for one another in that wild arena of calamities... Right was stamped underfoot, brutal power controlled everything with all its insolence; being predatory was virtually a privilege, for only those with sharp claws had a say... Struggling in beastly ways was the norm. Preying on each other was honorable. Might was right. The thought of justice was unimaginable; the weak suffered nightmares of oppression... Righteousness, innocence, and chastity were at their lowest, even worse than in our day. Neither the heart, nor the mind was of any concern; sound thinking and religious feelings were despised. The conscience was an alien idea of lost notions, pushed to some corner of the mind. The spirit was mistreated, and it crept along a few levels below biological life. Theft was popular, robbery was equal to chivalry, pillage was a sign of courage. Thoughts were miserable, feelings were wild, hearts were merciless, and horizons were pitch-black... He came at such a period, with the magnificent immensity of his heart which sufficed against everything. He came and cleaned the filth of the world in a single move. He cleared up the darkened horizons and revived hearts with the hope of light. He called to all mankind to behold a new day in the bright face of dawn. He raised the veil from people's eyes and let souls enjoy the pleasure of witnessing different things, things they had never seen before. He made the pulse of the mind follow the rhythm of the heart. He transformed various ravings in people into spiritual zeal.

When he came, the sincerest of smiles replaced the grief on the mourning faces. He came and oppression fell silent. The lamenting of the oppressed ceased, and feelings of justice in the hearts were revived. He came and halted the reign of brutal power, taught the transgressors a lesson, and unchained the tongue of the righteous.

If we are still able to talk about certain perfections in spite of so many nightmares and disasters, we owe it to the magnificent heavenly Book he offered to us, which is a collection of universal values. The feeling of seeking the good, beautiful, and humane in our hearts comes from the light he shed, the light with the color of infinity. The longing for eternal bliss we feel in our souls is from the light of faith he sparked in our souls.

Since knowing him, all of us have changed, everything has changed; we have comprehended that we have been created for eternity, we were meant for eternity. And then our ruined hearts turned into splendid gardens. Then our surroundings suddenly assumed the colors of Paradise. When Providence smiled at us and we took his side, all the monsters lying in wait failed, one by one. Wolves and jackals took shelter in their dens, with their tails between their legs. Snakes changed their attitude and become friends with the doves. Devilish fires were extinguished, one by one, and the devils moved to valleys of hopelessness; then an aura of spirituality began to make its presence felt.

O light that has illuminated our dark worlds, O rose that has turned worlds into perfumeries with your wonderful scent, your sudden departure, like a sunset in our hearts, has turned our mornings of hope into a pitch-dark night of grief. Visibility has been lost in a fog, and the roads are totally confused. A time has come when the mind has been diverted from your path to other valleys. Thoughts have totally refused to understand you and the monsters who lay in ambush for years have filled everywhere. They have attempted to obliterate your name from our hearts and make new generations forget you. These wicked efforts have entangled our derelict world in inauspiciousness and the fate of the community has become hunched in misery. We have failed to stand our ground; we could neither be as we were supposed to be, nor have we been able to reach our claimed destination. We have become detached from our spiritual roots and we have failed to interpret the matter and the world. We have let ourselves into the withering atmosphere of a dismal fall. As everybody ran to the horizons of their own world of thoughts, we have just remained immured where we were, in a chilling annihilation.

Now a frightening uncertainty in your world prevails; insights are narrow, thoughts are twisted, and feelings of renewal and revival are totally paralyzed. For years the blessed lands where you were born have lain completely barren; they bear no fruit now. Your beloved hometown is in silent protest at our faithlessness. Be it Damascus or Baghdad, they all produce anomalous births. Balkh and Bukhara are questing for nothing in valleys of emptiness. Konya is seeking consolation in folkloric performances. From one end to the other, the spirit of the great Andalusia is mourning the past. Istanbul goes through constant fluctuations in the claws of aimlessness. And an entire world is alone, orphaned, writhing in paroxysm, and tortured by time.

A black shadow has been cast over the magnificent meaning you brought. Now there is a terrible obstruction between you and our hearts, caused by heedlessness, ignorance, and lack of insight. In this eclipse that we are experiencing, we cannot see our surroundings nor make a sound evaluation, let alone utter a remark about the future. I cannot tell whether the souls to whom your light has not reached can be revived. Actually, how can revival be possible for the masses who do not assume their light, color, or style from you?

All of us have grimly watched the setting of your spirit behind the slopes of our hearts in an unhappy period. We were not able to do anything before that chilling sunset and we remained passive, presenting an example of complete helplessness. And then all the divine blessings, grace, peace, happiness, and the sweetest poems of the period of bliss ceased. In these days, when we long for your blessed face and character, grief is our portion, and silence is our part. In this unfortunate period, as we pass through pitch-black voids, the skies never look promising. The stars never wink at us. The sun and the moon never assume the color they had in your time. We see darkness around us constantly and are startled by the grunting of night creatures. You are not among us anymore, and the hissing of snakes and insects can be heard all around; the screaming of bats echoes everywhere. I cannot tell whether your heart is broken because of us—if that is ever possible—but there is one thing I know, we may have hurt you; indeed, to imply mere possibility in this phrase is nothing but a statement of hopefulness. However, if you do not grant us a kindness and honor our hearts, then we will be completely shattered, broken into pieces. And if you do not come and clear the smoke and dust on the face of our world, then we will suffocate in this heavy air, never to be revived again.

O most beloved one of our hearts, please let us be your host one more time. Set your throne upon our hearts and order us to do any service you wish. Please come and expel the darkness within us, make us feel the inspirations of your spirit in all our being and show us the way to a new revival. Come and disperse the shadows that grow worse every day with your lights that crown the sun and extinguish the fire of oppression and injustice that causes us all to suffer. Come and unlock the chains around the necks of these poor souls who are set on rancor, hatred, and enmity; enliven our hearts, which have been deprived of mercy and compassion, with the enthusiasm of love and tolerance. Come and make our spirits meet the bright light of the mind and hearts with the immensity of logic and reasoning; save us from alienation within our own selves.

After you left, some of us became entangled in reason and began to lose our way from the straight path. And some of us surrendered to sweet dreams and wasted time in various fancies; we were unable to delve into the depths of spiritual life and we could no longer understand the language of reason. We ignored reason and corrupted the world; we completely neglected our hearts and oversaw our own deaths.

O sun and moon of our dark nights, O sole guide of those who broke down on the way; you were not and are not born once, like we were. Every period is a time of sunrise for you, and our hearts are humble skylines for your rise; our wretchedness is an invitation to you, and we are looking forward to your light. Please have mercy on our crying hearts and come; shine upon our souls for the love of the Creator, do not abandon us nor burn our souls with the fire of being without you. We are not learned enough, nor do we have power to do goodness; our sins and transgressions are immense. What we offer you is not even equal to *merchandise of scant worth* (Yusuf 12:88)… There is no one left whose door we have not knocked on; those we cherished hopes about and those we ran to have always cheated us and left us halfway. We have neither the energy to walk nor to retain our present position. Given that you are the owner—there is no doubt about that—then why should the orchard be left untended? Even making such a call to you is another form of disrespect. Given that being at the command is your right, then who can dare to speak on behalf of that post!

O sultan of hearts, whose mercy comes ahead of his justice, we acknowledge that we have been oblivious and disrespectful of you, but you have seen worse before; even though you were hurt, you did not cut off your relations with those who were unfaithful to you. You even opened your hands and prayed for those who injured your head and broke your tooth. Taking their ignorance of who you are as an excuse, you did not invoke curses on them, and you did not say amen to this kind of wish either. You opened your bosom so much that even people like Abu Jahl became hopeful, and you related your every word and act to the immensity of the mercy of the Almighty. Even though our expectations have no right to be claimed, we have no doubt that all that you do is a consequence of your exemplary character.

O friend, so many springs have passed while we have been stuck in this fall, but we still follow in your tracks, even though we stumble. Come and cheer us on one more time; we are in a state in which your name can be heard all around by the fresh saplings of your orchard. The world is in desperate need of your light. Even though we cannot make the best journey with our broken wills and cracked hopes, we are always on the path. You are the beloved we are seeking, even though merely with our feelings; come and shine in us for a final time so that our hearts will be filled with light and the long nights that darken our horizons will vanish to be replaced by bright daylight.

Even though our eyes do not see the signs of your sunrise, your flavor, delight, and scent enrapture all of us even now. Come and lead us again, so that your light will be shed on our souls. You are, as Itri expressed, *"a date palm of Mount Sinai which casts no shadow; a sun filling the world, light from head to toe."* Your message, thought, horizons, and every aspect of you is pure light; remove the veil from over your face, let the world be filled with your light, and let your name be heard all around!

O exalted friend, these words I have uttered are not a poem of praise, nor are they a serenade; they are a lament without a rhythm, the essence of which is longing, the spirit of which is grief; they belong to your loyal follower, a recurring lament...

A BLESSED REGION'S YEARS OF ALIENATION

We are going through a strange period; light and darkness are intermingled, day and night move abreast; those drifting to death en masse are on one side, and those reviving on another as if woken by the Trumpet of Archangel Israfil. Breezes of spring are wafting on one side, storms of total destruction rage on the other... We see great thorns among roses and flowers and hear the crowing of ravens over the melody of nightingales; or we see only roses blooming and nightingales singing on them. Ravings of unbelief accompany breaths of faith, howls of denial are intermingled with proclamations of faith. Sometimes we are disturbed by grunting in the form of words, and sometimes we are relaxed by golden sounds reaching into our hearts like lullabies. Those who scatter the seeds of thorn bushes all around are countless; yet, those who feast others on the fruits of Paradise are no fewer. I think so many opposites have never been so close to one another before.

For years we have reached the morning and evening like the survivors of Atlantis, with the longing for that lost land and with our eyes on the inauspicious sunsets on our horizons. Sometimes we felt shaken, and sometimes we were enlivened with the hope that the values we had lost would simply return home. Now as well, sometimes dawning beauties whisper some things into our hopes, and this is followed by a windstorm like a cold spell in mid-March. Sometimes what has been done is destroyed; and the things which are not destroyed are shaken successively. In this continual pattern, those who run courageously replace the ones who unfortunately topple.

We sometimes feel joy by ascribing the fortunate happenings to the extra blessings and special bounties of God Almighty, and sometimes we feel bitter in the face of various troubles and writhe in disappointment, as we see the crude behavior of people whom we thought to be more mature than that, as we think about the coarseness and bigotry of the souls fixated on denial and unbelief, the faithlessness of friends, the peculiar attitudes of those who stand close but seem distant, and the continual inconsistency of those who waver. How could a people whose past is so sound and whose spiritual roots are so splendid become such a society of contradictions with these warped thoughts and in this condition! How could we have failed to understand and sold our soul to Mephistopheles, and sacrificed our heart for what is merely carnal! How we have let our physicality run wild by bridling our spirit! How we have disobeyed God and gained the stamp of rebellion on our foreheads!

Unfortunately we were in a daze that was incompatible with our character and were unable to see what was happening. Every single day we were bending and debasing ourselves more and more and going through successive disappointments which affected the hue and pattern of our collective spirit. Then our horizons narrowed, our faces darkened, our thoughts became warped, and our words turned to ravings; however, we remained unaware of this striking change.

There came a time when all of these misfortunes totally upset our stance. Fissures began to appear in the spirit of togetherness and unity. Individuals in society were scattered like the beads of a broken string. The people were manipulated until society was polarized. Grudge and hatred were fanned between different groups, and everyone began to hound each other. In time, society became completely ugly, and dark faces replaced shining ones. Dark voices began to rise everywhere. And then groups of people began to prey on one another, and the system set about crushing and grinding all of them. All that could be heard were the grunts of the oppressors or the laments of the oppressed. All this happened, is still happening, and seems likely to go on happening in future. It is certainly a very bitter and saddening picture. However, what made it worse was the fact that the great self-sacrificing figures with bleeding hearts through whom we hoped for a solution were muzzled.

We have no right to complain about the present picture for sure. On the other hand, it is unthinkable for believers who care about their society to overlook what is happening. Unfortunately, with a distorted understanding which has its roots in the very distant past, we corrupted religious life just as we corrupted ourselves. And we sacrificed the spirit of unity to our whims. Instead of leaving matters of logic to our reason, and then turning reason in the pull of our heart and spirit towards sublime notions, thereby adorning our hearts with knowledge of God, we just turned our backs on our faculties such as insight (*basira*), will (*irada*), consciousness, feeling, cognition, and spiritual intellect (*latifa al-Rabbaniya*[26]) and thus darkened both the corporeal and spiritual worlds. Now we turn in a different direction every day in yet another confusion, every day we become entangled in different fantasies and run from one alter to another. We constantly make mistakes when we try to explain something or when we bite our tongues and keep silent, thereby constantly causing new problems; and we do this again and again. We just cannot manage to organize ourselves, focus on a single objective, and in doing so turn to God wholeheartedly.

We are not truly aware that we have fallen, and we have never been so. Our determination to stand up is short-lived. Our thoughts are warped, and our will is cracking, our decisions are inconsistent, and we cannot shake off the alienation killing our souls. Sometimes we walk on paths that contradict our belief and ideals, sometimes we are overwhelmed by currents flowing against our own direction

---

[26] These Sufi concepts are explained in detail in the author's *Key Concepts in the Practice of Sufism* series.

of thought and drift into unknowns, and sometimes we are stabbed in the back by those whom we were following.

For years, such strange escapades have been our fate; we have been running in dry valleys in search of water. We have been letting our buckets down into dry wells. We sometimes sought sugar in wild cane, and sometimes wasted our lives by cultivating thorns. In spite of our rich cultural heritage which could satisfy entire worlds, we did not manage to free ourselves from bowing and scraping before others. Instead of strolling on the hillsides of our history, which have always resembled rose gardens, we kept being entangled in and scratched by others' thorns. In spite of the singing of nightingales in our gardens, we have been listening to the wearying cawing of crows.

Our collective nature and character seem to have become so deformed in recent years that now we are embarrassed to be ourselves; we turn our backs on the values we have held for several thousand years, and we deny—though not all of us—our own spiritual roots and historical dynamics. Instead of proclaiming our unfading magnificent historical heritage everywhere and letting everybody see its depths, we just listen to the disturbing growls of certain powers, and suffer from a certain inner sickness.

Since the day we lost our magnificent position in the international balance of states, the world has been run by unruly ones; the fate of humanity has been entrusted to the unscrupulous. Everywhere, looters have been looking out for new targets to ransack. The blessings of the earth are in the hands of the ungrateful. The idea of right and considerations of fairness and justice are reduced to cries for help occasionally uttered by the wronged. The feeling of mercy or compassion has simply disappeared from hearts. Feelings of faith, loyalty, and trust have become blunted; and it seems that honor, dignity and self-respect are forgotten.

For centuries we have been oblivious to our most vital values and have turned our faces completely away from the centuries-long cultural heritage. Furthermore we have corrupted the minds of the young with foreign perspectives which do not suit us at all, but which we gathered from different corners of the world and attempted to use to replace our cultural and religious values. Now these young people, most of whom have become aimless, are condemning their own values, insulting the national spirit and thought, trying to destroy every part of their ancient inheritance and heading toward "nothings" in different lanes divided into so many factions. In spite of all this, the number of those who correctly see and interpret what is going on is not small. However, most of these just keep biting their tongues as if they were muzzled and they remain in silent contemplation. Even though they sometimes speak up and take a few steps, they then draw even further back from where they previously stood in the face of a little pressure or a petty threat, and they just hang around waiting for surprise blessings to come. By behaving in this way, they either confuse reliance on God with passively expecting Him to make everything happen, or they become entangled in self-contradictions, or they contaminate their relations with God by failing to take a stance as they should, or failing to fulfill their obligations. Thus, they encourage the enemies of our people too. Instead of fulfilling the purpose for which they were given free will and becoming themselves, they become victims of their weaknesses and make themselves vulnerable to others' establishing their control over them.

For years, no matter how sound its past was, society has been left squirming with its heart and mind detached from each other; it can neither come up with a reasonable interpretation of the universe and what takes place in it, nor make a sound evaluation of social developments. It just gapes around and is carried here and there on different winds. To tell the truth, this lack of direction seems likely to continue until the moment we come to ourselves and once again interpret the whole of existence, events, and ourselves correctly, and once more express ourselves through a new analysis and synthesis. I wish we had been able to change this inverted course of fate! How I wish we could have taken a firm stance as becomes our position granted by Providence and fulfilled the due of what we were blessed with. It is so sad that we failed to do so. I even dare say that we are just occasionally squirming in our helpless inability to do anything in the face of events. We sometimes bury our suffering and sorrow in our bosoms and swallow it, and sometimes we burst into tears. But we always suffer heart-rending grief. In a situation like this, it is not possible for us to say that we have fulfilled our responsibility towards God Almighty or towards our people either.

I wish we could have kept our loyalty just this much. I wish we could have at least opened up to God and cried. We failed to do that and to preserve the thoughts that belong to us. We failed to turn to God with our whole being and open our hearts to Him. For years, we led an unfeeling life. But considering the position of our people, we should have had some stories from the heart to tell the entire world. In the world of the future, there should have been some colors from our looms of thought as well. We ought not to have submitted ourselves to a downcast mood of loneliness and inadequacy in this world. We should have found some others to share our sorrow and suffering, and walked hand in hand with them towards being ourselves.

It is still not too late; we have a world of opportunities before us. The number of those devoted to God is not so small. I think all that is left to do is to seize the reins in a firm grasp and set off with love and zeal, rely on God, knock on His door, open up in tears and say, "We have come." So now, to compensate in part for our having spent so much time laughing in a miserable condition, let us try to express ourselves with the feelings of our heart and our tears.

A SEASON TO WEEP

Time has always made this poor Zihni weep,
I went to the orchard, and saw the keeper weep,
Hyacinths are just wretched, roses sadly weep
Since the beloved nightingale left this orchard.

Zihni

Tears manifest feelings like sadness, joy, and compassion, which swell inside like clouds, and are expressed through the eyes. Worry, sorrow, eagerness, zeal, objectives, hopes, separation, reunion—perhaps more than all of these, what makes a person weep is awe and fear of God, particularly one with a wakeful heart who loves Him deeply. Other types of weeping are the outcomes of natural and ordinary conditions; they are not a result of opening up to God, and therefore are commonplace.

As for the cries triggered by sincere feelings and whose essence is based on faith and knowledge of God, they spring completely from awareness of God, sensing Him in everything, living with dreams of reunion at some unknown time, and trembling in awe and standing in His presence in the utmost reverence. This awareness is limited; very few fortunate ones have achieved it, and its continuity depends on their gaze reading Him in everything, sensing Him, demanding Him, knowing Him, and telling of Him. Those who know feel interest; when the interest grows deeper in the spirit, it turns into love, and in time this love becomes an irrepressibly passionate love of God. Now such people cannot remain still; they stride through deserts, like Majnun seeking Layla.[27] Such people are constantly eager to overcome their own remoteness

---

[27] A Sufi metaphor for an initiate seeking God.

from Him. They keep seeking signs and traces which tell of God, sometimes converse with creation, and sometimes interpret things and events as if they were letters from Him, smell their scent, and try to feel them. And sometimes, they are moved by these messages, and find relief in tears. And sometimes, they are entranced by heralds who tell of Him and always breathe with deep eagerness. This is the condition of those who try to feel and sense the Artist through the art, awakening to the Owner of all beauties through the beauties they encounter, lending an ear to everything that recalls Him and listening to Him in reverence, those who try to lead their lives like an embroidery of love being worked, feeling great closeness and love for everything because of Him.

Also at the times of separation and reunion with friends and relatives people's eyes are filled with tears, perhaps not for reasons as deeply felt as in reverence to God; this is also a type of weeping, however the value of every cry is measured in the life to come according to the depth of feeling and thought of the sufferer. Those who open up to God and cry out of feelings of awe and self-accounting, or those who try to control the storm for the reason given by the poet Fuzuli,

You say you are a lover, then do not complain of the affliction of love;
By complaining, do not make others informed of your affliction

are the loyal servants at the door of the Beloved. Such people keep their secret so faithfully that they are even jealous of their own eyes. Both their cries and silences are sound and meaningful.

On the other hand, forced acts of weeping which do not emanate from the heart are an unpleasant sight, disrespect for real tears, and deceitful. Therefore, such forced efforts to cry only make the devil happy and this means nothing but spoiling by pretentiousness a potion with a potential to extinguish hellfire and wasting it.

Weeping in a tone of discontentment and complaint in the face of misfortune and calamity is forbidden; whining with anxiety about the future is a disease of the spirit, lamenting what has been lost is in vain and a waste of tears.

The grief of the Prophet Jacob for his sons Joseph and Benjamin arose from the feeling of fatherhood and compassion; who knows, maybe the crying of that noble prophet came out of his seeing them as hope for the future and out of concern for their rank before God. If this is so—as we accept it to be—then these kinds of cries are not something to be avoided. On the other hand, the feigned crying of Joseph's brothers before their father was trickery and deception. When the time came, Joseph would forgive them and say, *"No reproach this day shall be on you; indeed, He is the Most Merciful of the merciful"* (Yusuf 12:92). And his brothers would respond, *"God has indeed preferred you above us, and certainly we were sinful."*

Crying for the sake of God is the sounding out of the love cherished for Him. One who has fire in the heart will have tears in the eyes; a person with eyes as dry as deserts does not have life within.

Sadness and tears are the most important characteristic of God's prophets. The Prophet Adam wept for a lifetime. The weeping of Prophet Noah was like a flood of lamentation. Prophet Muhammad, the Pride of Humanity, peace be upon him, always reflected the poetry of his feelings in tears. In this respect, it would not be a mistake to call him a prophet of sadness and tears. On one occasion, he cried until the morning while repeating the verses, *"if You punish them, they are Your servants; and if You forgive them, You are the All-Glorious with irresistible might, the All-Wise,"* (Maeda 5:118) and *"they (the idols) have indeed caused many among humankind to go astray. So, he who follows me is truly of me; while he who disobeys me, surely You are the All-Forgiving, All-Compassionate"* (Ibrahim 14:36). When the Archangel Gabriel conveyed the reason for this weeping to God Almighty, He relieved the Prophet with the glad tidings that He would not upset the Prophet about the community.[28]

---

[28] Muslim, *Iman*, 346.

God's Messenger led his life in a continual state of sadness and reflection, most often in contemplation and then weeping. Even though occasional glad tidings made him joyful, he would most often open up like a nightingale and weep. A nightingale cries and screams, even when it lands on the rose. It is virtually created for mourning. On the other hand, crows have no such worry, and ravens only raise their voices near food.

Sadness and weeping is the usual state of the lovers of God, and mourning day and night is the shortest path to Him. Those who reproach the lover for his or her tears can be considered to have revealed their own roughness. Understanding nothing now of the hearts burning with longing, they will spend their lives in longing and grief in the other world.

The Qur'an often draws attention to people with fire in their hearts and tears in their eyes and always counsels that they be taken as examples.

In appreciation of eyes which cry for the sake of the good of the soul, the realm of Hereafter, and out of awe of God or repentance for sins, the Qur'an says, *those who were endowed before it with knowledge fall down on their faces in prostration when the Qur'an is recited to them... and it increases them in humility and a feeling of awe* (Isra 107–109), and takes the tears shed for the sake of God as a gift with which to beseech His mercy.

After God commends and praises different prophets in the chapter of Mary for their special merits, He concludes by mentioning their common characteristic of weeping: *...when the All-Merciful's Revelations were recited to them, they would fall down, prostrating and weeping* (Maryam 19:58).

The Qur'an praises those who received the first signs in the earlier revelations to the Messenger of God and then who are moved— and thus whose faith reaches the degree of certainty—while listening to the message sent to the Final Prophet; it underlines the importance of tears in the sight of God by stating, *When they hear what has been sent down to the Messenger, you see their eyes brimming over with tears because of what they know of the truth...* (Maeda 5:83).

Similarly, the Qur'an highlights another group of heroes of tears in the verse, *...when they came to you to provide them with mounts, and you said, "I cannot find anything whereon to mount you," they returned, their eyes overflowing with tears in sorrow that they could not find anything to spend,* (Tawba 9:92) and consoles their broken hearts with divine acclaim.

As well as reminding us of the fact that true weeping is a condition particular to godly people, the Qur'an also issues a warning about those who spend their lives in amusement, taking this life as play and entertainment; here the Qur'an places a different emphasis on the importance of crying in *So let them laugh little and weep much, in recompense for what they have been earning* (Tawba 9:82).

The Qur'an underlines the same fact in tens of verses and different ways and counsels us to adopt a stance that suits our position.

The blessed purveyor of the Qur'an, the Prophet, with his brilliant soul, kept his life in line with these insistent counsels from the Qur'an. From time to time, he would show his Companions the three steps to ascent, saying, *"Glad tidings to those who control their carnal selves! Glad tidings to those who keep their homes large and convenient (for guests)! Glad tidings to those who shed tears for their mistakes!"*[29] and thus he would invite them to join his company. He would also turn the attention of his Companions to the dreadful things beyond the physical realms with statements such as, *"If you knew what I know, you would laugh little but cry much."*[30]

He would counsel his Companions to weep and cry, draw attention to the fact that tears untainted with hypocrisy and shed in awe of God could be a shield against divine punishment: *"There two types of eyes which hellfire will not touch in the afterlife: one is the eye*

---

29   Munziri, *at-Targib wa't-Tarhib*, 4/116.
30   Bukhari, *Kusuf*, 2; Muslim, *Fadail*, 134.

shedding tears in awe of God, and the other is the one which watches out for the enemy at the frontiers."[31]

Another time he emphasized the same meaning in different words: "*It is not possible for milk which has come out of a breast to go back where it came from; it is equally impossible (concerning the divine practice of God) for one who cries and moans in awe of God to enter Hell.*"[32] Thus, he emphasized the value of tears in God's sight. And if this crying happens somewhere away from other people and seen only by God ... Indeed, I must confess that I do not know a criterion to appreciate how excellent such a thing is.

Everywhere and all the time the Prophet reminded people of such things and he was already far ahead of what he said. During his prayer, a sound similar to the creaking of grindstones was heard from his bosom, to the sound of his inner weeping.[33]

The Prophet asked Ibn Masud to recite to him verses from the Qur'an. When Ibn Masud came to the verse meaning, *How then, will it be (with people on the Day of Judgment) when We bring forward a witness (a prophet) from every community, and bring you (O Messenger) as a witness against all those (whom your Message may have reached)?* (Nisa 4:41), the Prophet signed him to stop. Ibn Masud reports, "When I turned to him, I saw that he was shedding tears."[34]

While he shed tears, his most distinguished Companions did not remain impassive for sure. They also cried and sometimes their crying grew into a chorus of woe and weeping. When the Prophet reminded his Companions of the verses meaning, "*Do you then deem this Discourse strange? And do you laugh and not weep (in consideration of your recalcitrance and sinfulness)?*" (Najm 53:59–60), all of them started to weep and sigh. Then the Prophet, who was moved by this scene, joined them in shedding tears. Seeing the Prophet crying touched the Companions even further and they completely

---

31 Tirmidhi, *Fadail al-Jihad*, 12.
32 Tirmidhi, *Fadail al-Jihad*, 8; Nasai, *Jihad*, 8.
33 Abu Dawud, *Salat*, 157; Nasai, *Sahw*, 18.
34 Bukhari, *Fadail al-Qur'an* 33; Muslim, *Salat al-Musafirin* 247.

abandoned themselves to tears.[35] Those blessed people already cried and wept constantly; sometimes with the joy of faith and knowledge of God, sometimes in fear of punishment in the Hereafter, and sometimes at the darkening of the horizon, they would weep and turn to the door of divine mercy with cries of supplication.

As a matter of fact the reckoning of our prayers which reach God quickest is largely related to our inner yearnings and tears, since it is not possible to find anything else that reflects the feelings of the heart more swiftly and purely than tears. The forces of sin are put to rout where heartfelt sobs wave their flags. Wakeful hearts are relieved with the pleasant breezes of divine approval touching their consciences.

Those who spend their lives in woe and weeping for the sake of God are considered by the inhabitants of heavens to be nightingales of loyalty and divine love. When they start to sing, all the spirit beings hush and start listening to them. Given that true crying is a waterfall springing from the heart and emerging through the eyes, then one should direct it toward eternity and offer it to the Almighty Lord in the utmost secrecy; it should not be contaminated through showiness, turning a waterfall to overcome Hellfire into the acid of falsehood.

We are living in a world which has lost its light and is covered with dust and smoke on all sides. We all need to turn our eyes down on the ground in humility, contemplate our transgressions and sins, and then let out such a wail like a nightingale that all the inhabitants of the heavens hasten to this feast of weeping with shining torches in their hands. These days when the flames around us are so far out of control, I think it is high time we dissolved into tears. Since tears are a potion that breaks all kinds of devilish spells, instead of enjoying ourselves with the coarsest merriment everywhere we go, we should try to relieve our minds and put an end to suffering and lamentation with our tears.

---

35 Bayhaqi, *Shuab al-Iman*, 1/489.

According to friends of God, tears bear the secret of becoming life for lifeless corpses, like the breath of Jesus, and everywhere they flow they bring life, like the water of life. Those who deepen with their crying the grottos of their night worship which are closed to all but God, and make their souls listen to the music of entreaty will certainly be revived tomorrow if not today, and continue to breathe life everywhere they go.

Our prayer rugs dried out long ago. For years, our ears have strained after the screams of the heart. Our atmosphere is as dry as deserts. It seems that we do not feel the burning of the hearts that burn with grief. Our faces resemble blocks of ice, and our glances are totally devoid of meaning. There is no trace of agonizing pain in our bosoms. And our expressions are not convincing. This kind of heedlessness can only make it very difficult for us to walk toward the future and continue our existence.

Ever since the day our tears ceased to flow, the springs of blessings from the sky have also dried up in a sense. Rains of inspiration do not fall anymore; roses and tulips do not grow. The lights from the sky flicker and the occasional winds are feeble. The inhabitants of the heavens are thirsty for woe and weeping. The residents of the heavens are awaiting tears to form clouds. As the poet Zihni expressed it,

> *Rose and hyacinth taken by the thorns*
> *Snakes have captured the throne of Solomon*
> *Spiritual joys are now woe and groans*
> *Once an age of bliss, now a time to mourn.*

Who knows, maybe the celestial beings are waiting for our tears before they take charge? Possibly, when we wail and cry about the troubles surrounding us on all sides, the horizons of the heavenly realms will fill with clouds laden with merciful rains, and as they see our sins, transgressions, and faults drifting away on the stream of our tears, they will be filled with joy and pour down on us in compassion. I guess that sometimes heavenly beings—just as we wipe our faces with the rosewater offered during gatherings in honor of the Blessed Birth (of the Prophet)—wipe their faces with our tears, which stand for the breaths of grieving hearts, and they take our tears as a valuable gift offered to them.

Our sins and transgression are as huge as mountains, yet our regrets and their accompanying tears are mere show, and there is no trace of suffering in our hearts. Our crying and weeping are mostly for things of this world. In this condition, we need nothing but tears of regret to purify us from the dirt of centuries. Probably, it is only through these tears that we can reach the door of repentance and rebuild our wasted life.

Prophet Adam's lapse, which he took to be as huge as Mount Everest, melted and disappeared through his tears. Like incense giving off a pleasant scent all around as it burned, he burned within and groaned with regret, and thus was exalted to an honorable rank, like a shrine to be revered by angels. And when the time came and his suffering was completed, the dawn of every new day broke in the hues of the decree of his forgiveness.

As far what falls to us after so many sins, transgressions, and the consequent suffering, I think we need to seek times when we are away from others' eyes, hide behind the veil of the night, prostrate ourselves before God and shed tears... for our faithlessness, for not being able to be truly sincere, for constantly zigzagging on our path, for not fulfilling the due of our position, for not being able to take a sound stance as becomes what we are blessed with, and for the offences of others who follow our bad example; we should weep in such a way that even the heavenly beings who constantly weep will shed tears for our cries from now on.

We have failed to preserve the position that was granted to us; we have failed to take a determined and conscious stance in pure sincerity. We have let go each other's hands, we have lost what is dear to us, roses have been struck by fall, and nightingales have started to cry mournfully. Fountains have ceased, rivers dried up. Thorns have appeared, and ravens are crowing all around. We should say something with the tongue of our heart, and we should put an end to this drought by pouring potions of tears upon our longings and emotions.

Our Creator has directed us toward the goal of living in accordance with our potentials by endowing us with blessings like a body, life, feeling, consciousness, cognition, and so on. But we have sacrificed everything to our fancies and withdrawn far back from our ordained position, as far back as we could possibly retreat; in retreating we damaged our capacity to live as human beings and we were also damaged. From now on at least, should we not show determination to lead our life in the direction of our heart!

Now come, let us sing laments in payment for our heedless joy until today. Let us be concerned a bit and bid farewell to leading a life oriented toward carnality and try to sense the other hues of life as well. Let us speak of concerns, listen to concerns, and seek ways of being close to the One Who listens to those who are concerned.

The good days of our life have mostly been wasted. Now we see on the horizon the signs of the night after the day of our life. What falls to us now is to light a torch for the long night after this life. From now on at least, we need to come to ourselves, free ourselves of this confusion, turn to our essence, and express the longing in our hearts through tears. And we should know that in the sight of God, nothing has ever fallen on this earth dearer to Him than genuine tears. The drops falling on earth today will soon turn into beautiful greenery all around. Come, in this steppe drier than deserts let us be the cupbearer of tears for everyone and serve all around us with a banquet of the freshest fruits we can offer, with the lyrics of our emotions and the melody of our tears.

THE WALLS AROUND PEACE HAVE
COME DOWN

Today, almost all of us lead our lives in constant haste and anxiety; we drift from one delirious state into another; we experience panic in our enterprises and we shake with the fear at the terrifying surprises that could be awaiting us two steps away. We are unable to produce new ideas; we do not have any serious plans for the future. We move in a strange manner like sleep walkers. Our responses in the face of unexpected events are nothing but rough reactions. What we are doing—or what we seem to be doing—against the dreadful destructive strategies of the enemies of our society that date back many long years, is no more than a struggle to survive. If only we could have conducted this struggle according to its own rules at least.... I am not willing to confess it, but future generations will probably note our failure even in observing the rules of this struggle.

Consider this fact for instance: decisions concerning matters that will keep our society busy for a lifetime are mostly taken by others. Trying to find a way out of these decisions—taken completely out of our own control—or wondering how we can benefit from moves initiated by others or how we can prevent those moves from being to our disadvantage, we frantically change our state, run from one shelter to another, what we do one day we undo the next, and we waste our lives in an endless cycle of doing and undoing. And, of course, the naïve masses are confused. While some keep losing credit, others keep losing altitude. We are almost pinned down by our lack of judgment, our heedlessness, and ignorance with a force stronger than gravity. Those who hold power are mostly callous and insensitive; masses are running after the sense they lost God knows when; healthy thought is assailed by an oppressive bombardment of disrespect. Mass media organs whose duty is to educate, enlighten, and direct society toward high human ideals are completely heedless. They welcome anything without any sense of responsibility; they keep snarling the very darkest things and playing with people's honor, dignity, and decency. Every day they come up with yet another new clamor of doom and gloom. By describing and displaying the false temptations of this world, they arouse decadent desires in people with previously pure feelings and thoughts. There are some among them that continually broadcast immorality as if they were programmed to create corruption and disorder; they bypass honor, dignity, and morality for the sake of ratings and do things that make one ashamed of being human.

Society reaches every morning and evening in the shadow of the signs of the apocalypse, almost in expectation of the trumpet blast announcing its arrival. Our peace and tranquility have become naught but a dream. Our collective spirit and thought, which were our main shelter until today, have become twisted and deformed. Our hopes have become more tattered than they have ever been. Our willpower is crazed with a network of cracks. Our determination is totally paralyzed. And as a society we continually pass through delirious states. We have become so detached from our essence that if we were to meet our own spirit round the corner, we might not even recognize it.

We have never been so alienated from our own values in any period of history. We have never left our spirit so hungry, thirsty, and deprived of air. Nowadays, different noises keep coming at us from all sides, but we are unable to hear among them the voice of our spirit that makes us ourselves. We are in such a state of bewilderment, terror, or rather confusion that we are unable to see what we are supposed to be. I think it will not be possible for us to be saved from this deadly chaos until we wash away our mental and spiritual dirt with the clear flow of our own belief and thought.

Surrounded by strange, shrill noises, by shows tempting people to self-alienation, and by nightmarish troubles that stab our hearts, take strength from our helplessness and make our souls lament, we go through shock after shock, writhe in pain, keep swallowing helplessly, and feel our spirit grow more and more corroded every day.

We certainly cannot ignore certain hopeful voices we hear and promising developments we witness from time to time, but in order for these weak voices—whose existence is entrusted to a long term process to ring out like a powerful call—and for these formations to set about a process of flourishing with our inner world, we need people dedicated to service for God, who possess sound hearts, strong character and determination, vigorous souls like noble horses which gallop flat beyond the limits of their strength, and people of insight who show active endurance. In my opinion, thanks to the wholehearted volunteers who possess these qualities, we will be able to free ourselves of the unfortunate troubles which have for years been preventing us from being ourselves by insinuating their way into our feelings and thoughts and tarnishing them. Then, as a whole society, we will be able to regain our own nature, character, and purity of our souls engrained in true belief in God.

Once, we were one of the purest, clearest, cleanest, and most well-mannered societies of the world; in some periods, we were the highest of all. In every part of society there prevailed a serious love for truth, keenness for research, eagerness for knowledge, an ethics of justice, and a feeling of compassion and mercy, all of which were based on faith and depended on devotion to God for their continuation. Both the individual and society were reflective and mindful of God in every moment of their lives; they would embrace everybody and everything with compassion and accept prime responsibility for the equilibrium in the world as a necessity of being God's vicegerent. Sometimes, they would shower like rains everywhere, without omitting any place, sometimes they would run like rivers, become life and flow; a day would come when they would boil like the seas and inspire awe all around; and a time would come when they would appear with various hues and fragrances like roses and flowers, filling those who beheld them with delight. There was always a grace and elegance which found its meaning with our society renewing itself with a different flavor, different accent, and different taste, while retaining all the specialties of its essence and evoking heavenly feelings in consciences. The ongoing chaos all over the world and some crude noises rising here and there would change rhythm with the peace and abiding security emanating from their climate, slow down, and virtually fade away with that atmosphere. In this world, where life was always experienced as a melody, even the most unpleasant creaks became inaudible. Silence overwhelmed as if imperatively, a heavenly security, and an air of immense peace pervaded everywhere. So the people of this fortunate land often withdrew to one or two steps behind their dreams and entered a deep otherworldly trance; they lived all past and present times concurrently in that deep blue climate of their faith and their hopes, and rained smiles all around them in appreciation of their own condition.

Occasionally, opposing winds would pierce this silvered atmosphere, discolor this azure nature, and the environment would pale a little. However, thanks to the general atmosphere's being open to heavenliness, even the fiercest winds would immediately turn to breezes, colors would reflect the spring, and everything would regain its spiritual meaning. In that world, neither constant heedlessness of the divine and the flippancy springing from that, nor constant suffering and crying could be heard. Even if some unpleasant events tore through our peace and serenity from time to time, they did not last long. They would finish as they began, and everything would settle back into place again. Then the atmosphere of our nation and society would return to its wonderful state, it would assume an otherworldly color open to the heavens and to those deserving of heaven. It was such that all the realms of the unseen were sensed almost as if they would appear before the beings and events in the corporeal world and they would whisper such secrets to our souls. And then these magical inspirations would become a depth of our inner world and make us speak in their own accent. As these heartfelt feelings recurred, in time they brought our souls a new perspective befitting our characters, and they knocked at the door of spirituality for us. They did this in such a way that we would sometimes take the place in which we found ourselves to be part of the heavens extended upon the earth, and we would think ourselves inhabitants of that realm of delights.

The secret key to our riches and to the treasuries of divine graces overflowing from our spirit and hearts was our faith, and the secret to its staying ever fresh was our good deeds and sincerity. Believers felt in their hearts the ease brought by these heavenly inspirations and enjoyed the same awe that celestial beings feel.

A flood of light streaming from living up to the belief, the divine scripture, and the religion at this level would almost all the time wave with a magic breaking the power of all these opposite winds; it enwraps us like a divine light showering down from a spiritual decree, and it would affect the sight, hearing, and sensing, and evaluations of our entire soul system. In such cases when we were able to remain open to the levels of the spirit, we would see the world we gaze on as an exhibition of divine art, read the universe and events like a book, see all people honored with the same blessings and all living or non-living beings submitted to us as our friends and companions, and we thought we were in the corridors of Paradise with the deep delight that all of these made us feel.

Then, a day came while we were walking with these blessings, free from every kind of foreboding, we were unexpectedly ambushed by demons. They poured acid on our hearts and made our horizons murky. They unsighted us and deprived us of the exhibition we had been viewing and the book we had been reading. They stole our sun and darkened the face of our moon, cut the bonds of our stars and made them all fly into the abyss, and they made our bright world dark by spreading pitch on the face of everything.

In that period, our carnal self ascended to the throne of the soul. Our hearts were mortgaged to the devil. Monuments of fancy replaced our Creator. Dignity and morality were stamped underfoot. Feelings of shame and innocence gave way to indecency. Disrespect became the most common thing. Everywhere turned into a fair of filth and ugliness. Manners and grace were presented as worthless relics from the past. They first made souls forget faithfulness, loyalty, and devotion to values; and then these were erased from the dictionary.

All those previous orchards and gardens were destroyed, roses and flowers went into mourning, all around began turning into desert again. Thorny plants grew where once hyacinths were. Nightingales hushed, and it was the time of crows. As snakes and creeping things moved around freely, doves were confined to cages.

It was at this period when everything was at its nadir that public-spirited people began feel palpitations in their hearts, high-spirited ones became even more anxious, and the suffering of the heedful turned to agony…. This situation evoked in almost everybody a wish to journey toward being themselves. And these were the signs auguring the end of the hiatus that had lasted several centuries and the end of the idle stumbling.

Nowadays, there is zeal in a great many souls, and hearts have the desire to seek; in every valley there is a drove of thinkers with flurries of thoughts… in every region there is almost a celebration of birth. After that dreadful fall and that chilling, centuries-long silence, the time must have come for us to say something to the world, since we have had much to tell, and the season to tell it has arrived.

So the decline of several centuries that we have left behind has aroused such zeal in public-spirited souls that I think that even if our present situation had been much worse, the lesson we have learned would still be enough to make us rise and come to ourselves again, and this is at the same time a good source of motivation. We could say that the many long years of inertia and weariness are vacating their place to be replaced by an ardor for activity. The continual waves of negative events and successive hindrances that we have been undergoing have been more or less causing us to rediscover ourselves. So much so that rather than the present time, we have come to talk about the near or distant future and to live with dreams of tomorrow. We have begun to receive glimpses from the things that some people had always aspired to attain but failed to do so, inspiring us with the possibility of a true dawn, and this was awakening us to a new morning. Maybe the sun had not risen yet, but it was clear that the horizon was heralding daybreak.

We lost yesterday, but tomorrow is still before us. Now it is time to concentrate on the future with complete metaphysical tension and wait for the new gift that time has in its womb. In my opinion, those who failed to make good use of yesterday are not to be considered losers, given that the agony of what they have lost have recovered them and they have prepared for the morrow. We will wait and see what the night still has to offer before the sunrise!

THOSE WERE THE DAYS

As the years pass by, O Muhammad!
Months are, to us, turned to Muharram!
What a sunny night was the evening;
Alas! It too turned into a night of grief!
....
For the love of God, O Innocent Prophet!
Do not leave Islam so desolate,
And us so oppressed.

Mehmet Akif

Y ou were the one who once filled our hearts; everything was
so magical and beautiful with your presence. Nevertheless,
certain discontinuities were also experienced along the way
and there were times when conduct was ungracious, manners were
coarse, and voices and breaths were snarls; but all these shortcomings would immediately be wiped away by the light and breeze
from your world, and only you and your colorful atmosphere
would start to emerge as if in a reverie on the horizons of thought
and sense. The fading of the horizons to black, or the entwining of
souls with palpitations would seem a call for you to rise in hearts:
Whenever we were downhearted, your shade would rise over the
hills of our hearts like a full moon, obliterating all gloom. Every
time we were stuck in any kind of problem or troubled by ourselves, as if that state of self-oppression we were in was an invitation to your light, the warmth and soothing quality of your private
world would be immediately felt from all around, and we would be
immersed in the lights coming from eternity. The breezes would be
impregnated with your fragrance; the benefits of your climate

would pour on us like waterfalls, and we would become as cool as if we had bathed in the lights coming from beyond.

After almost every break, no matter how short it may be, we would say, "Shame on us, for not realizing how much we were without him," and we would find you in our hearts fresh and anew. After each faltering, each deviation, or gloom, the All-Compassionate would return you to us, and we would hear your voice and breath, your light and fragrance with all our hearts, and we would hear the captivating accent of your message; as if we were on a magical balloon, we would be liberated from gravity, feeling an air of progress toward the eternity in our souls. With the magic of that air, we would escape from our contaminated atmosphere and turn into celestial beings, such that, whenever we looked into our souls, we would feel a light, a hope, a relief emanating from your luminous world, knowing ourselves to be in your cordial presence since you were always there with us, and everything was so gorgeous with your presence.

You meant both the past, the future and the present for us; it was as if you were always with us with your enchanting stance transcending time. You would stand there in your era of light, yet embrace our day, give indications for the future, and make your voice heard at all times. Our bosoms were your summer palace; you would live in our hearts, have us live like you, disperse our palpitations as if you were singing lullabies softly for us in that sacred atmosphere of yours, warmer than the arms of our mothers and so comforting us all. Mostly, we would surrender to the charm of your spiritual peace and wander in the eras you had crowned with your light, observing the historical glories we had once achieved as your community; we would feel as if we had once more found the values we had lost or abandoned, cheer up like joyful children, then those gentle and spectacular days flowing from you would blossom in our memories like flowers. As a whole nation we would feel like we were suckling milk from the breasts of the Age of Light; and then, those rusty and dirty worlds of ours would glitter again; pieces of our broken, torn, and uncontrolled daydreams would come together, and times enlightened by you would flow into the days, hours, and minutes we had been living in, whispering to us the color, pattern, and accent of real life.

Whatever others who are not nourished from the same source as us may drink, we would almost always feel pleasures that nobody else felt; we would blink our eyes, and, as if we were in Paradise, we would get almost everything we reached for, we dreamt of, wished, or wanted, and it was as if we were always strolling in the realm of dreams. Yes, that is the way it should be since there was you inside ourselves; time, space, and everything associated with them were friendly to us.

Whenever we would establish contact with you in our hearts, your harmonious, spectacular, and radiant world would immediately start to emerge like a reverie over our ordinary states and thoughts, and your mysterious life adventure, stirring our feelings and emotions to overflow, would take us from where we were to the avenue by which we would reunite with you; by the same road, it would lead us eventually to the gates of God, and lay cushions like the sofas of Paradise for us in the ceremonial halls beyond spatial dimensions, providing our hearts with beauties comparable to our most beautiful daydreams. At those mystical times when we were with you, we would recall many more extraordinary things, experience great surges of pleasure and delight, rest in the cheer and joy of existence, and say repeatedly, "Indeed, this is the life." At those times, we were in your protective shade, aware of existence and nonexistence! The spirit and meaning distilled from your deep blue climate were our essence and life; we would live with them, go on our daily activities with them, surmount all the obstacles and reach all the summits we wished to reach with them; then, we would walk without pausing towards the most sacred of all targets: to win God's consent, and to make your name heard worldwide, your name which we consider as a means for His pleasure. With breaths as soft as silk, always soaring high like birds, caressing everything and everybody like a gentle breeze, from time to time turning into rain in the bosom of clouds, and then descending all around as a sparkling shower, we would effervesce with life at every moment. In those radiant days and hours when we lived to our heart's content and would say, "This is the life," our sun used to rise and set in harmony with you; days used to pass brightly like your face; nights used to sing to us from your black side-locks; and our pulses would always beat in harmony with the rhythms of your heart. We would rest our minds by thinking of you; our anxieties would be dispersed by taking shelter under your shade; and thus, we would get the taste of life, which we had never experienced before, and the endless joyful adventures of existence by being with you. We would read in your life adventure which was linked to the heavens, the invincible power of faith, that being a Muslim means being a hero, that fidelity involves priceless assets, and that chastity and innocence are angelic qualities.

You were the one who uttered the mysteries from beyond the heavens, and described lights flowing from the beyond, connections between this world and the afterworld, the expectations, dreams, and needs of humanity and the eternities promised in this matter. When your messages fell onto our ears, we would feel as if you were among us, as if your voice touched our inner selves, and we would observe the radiant snapshots of your luminescent life through our vision, and interpret the entire creation in you with all its particular content. The generations raised in your training, your style, and your system have been enthused and they have shuddered year after year in the waves of the deepest, most colorful, most charming, and most striking of the messages they heard from you; their faith has reached perfection—to the extent that unbelief, for them, does not have the slightest possibility—in proportion to their connection with you; their love turned into waterfalls; and they reached as far as the spiritual ones with a flood of deepest love and ardor.

Who knows what endeavors and efforts were invested so that the following generations over centuries would long to hear and love you this much and feel your message, which was the purpose of your existence? What consultations were held and what pains were taken! These yielded their fruits when it was the season; and then, there was you in every act, in every heart; and every minute, every second spent with you was auspicious. Your lights were continually pouring over our heads and flowing into our souls, and giving us delightful sensations! You were promising happiness to those who followed, replying to their wishes for eternal happiness; in return, their sentiments were running high at the thought that even more bright days would come in the future, and they were almost living a new Age of Happiness at the joy of being led by you.

We human beings were created weak, destitute, and needy with many expectations: We expected to have peace of heart, we sought fancies of happiness pertaining to this world as well as to the afterlife; we had dreams of eternity and eternal happiness and pursued what seemed to be beyond our capacity. With your coming and your luminous messages we were provided with blessings exceeding our expectations. We were like the dead before you arrived; but we were revived with your prophethood as if we heard the sound of the Trumpet.

In the past, you were within our hearts, and our days were real days; now, even though those bright days have not perished completely, they have lost their vividness and faded greatly. Our sorrow is like Jacob's and our hopes are as high as his; we all live by dreams of those bright days when you will rise again on our horizons, and we wait through the morning and the evening in excitement at your return as promised. Every year, your birth reminds us of this, and we feel as if we have drunk many cups full of the elixir of hope, and we are unable to be as grateful to the All-Compassionate as we ought for blessing the people of this age with you.

In recent past, those who broke away from you were lost. Those who went away ruined themselves. It is a fact that we all experienced estrangement to some extent; yet moving away from you took different forms, and so did losing you. Now, though it is late, we express our repentance for such estrangement, and we wish to return to your bosom, warmer than a mother's embrace. We are ashamed, and we are embarrassed; yet we have a firm belief that your wishes are acceptable to God. If only we had never broken off from you in any way; if only we had never separated from you and never been deprived of the lights coming from you and your world and meaning pouring into our souls; and if only we had been able to keep your persuasive face fresh and alive inside ourselves! Alas! Knowingly or unknowingly, we have been separated, and we have turned our backs on ourselves. Now, while following various prescriptions for deliverance, if only we could think about what we have lost! No, once again, we have been deceived by the tricks of Harut and Marut,[36] and we have been defeated by Satan once again. Yet, we had times when your shade lay over us and we could challenge all devils. While all around was fall, days and nights were like spring to us. Our years, months, and days were stolen, and we were transformed into the victims of time. Saying, "It is always darkest before the dawn," we are waiting for the auspicious times when this pitch darkness will be torn by the light.

---

36 Two angels who were sent to the Children of Israel during their life of exile in Babylon in order to teach them some occult sciences so that they might be protected against sorcery. See Baqara 2:102 for further information.

THE ENTIRE COSMOS IS A MIRROR
TO THE DIVINE

Everything in this universe is a mirror pointing to God Almighty, like an articulate language telling of Him, and a tune singing His Name. Human beings, things, and the whole of existence always reflects Him and bears witness to Him in their sounds and silences, acts and positions, in their beings and the fruits they yield. In their manners and stances they allude and point to Him. They are like shadows emanating from His existence in their weave, pattern, and accents.... Let those who cannot see fail to see; those who can see with their insight read His signs in everything, and listen to such sounds and words from His different manifestations. If hearts are open to Him and eyes can see beyond corporeality—this may not be to the same degree in everyone—whenever we look at existence as if we were reading it like a book, whenever we visit the exhibition of this earth and set ourselves to gazing at it, we find everything in it as mesmerizing as in dreams. Those who do not or cannot look at things and events in the Name of the Creator cannot feel this charm, underlying meaning and content. They cannot see the beauty, harmony, grace, and the underlying purpose, will, and wisdom behind all of these... They cannot feel the light, knowledge, love and vigor flowing from them into our souls.

However, all things are under a mysterious spell all the time. Nature sways like a flower bed. Rays of light gently descend as if being poured down on our heads with compassion. Breezes caress us with a new grace at every moment. And the winds blow with a mixture of scents.

In the sight of someone who has managed to adopt the right perspective, everything living or non-living points to God with its manner and appearance; as things smile at us, they make allusions to Him, presenting ranks of pictures of meanings which belong to Him. They open up to our gaze entrancing vistas and let our souls listen to choruses of the most delightful sounds. All of existence is enlivened in our eyes as if it were feeling the joy of reunion. We join the same rhythm at times, we enjoy the rapture as far as we are capable... and we remember Him in every breath we draw and release. As our vision become clearer, we see the hues appearing and hear the sounds echoing around us differently. We interpret every act and every sound very differently as if we were able to understand the tongues of all things. From the blades of grass and the trees swaying around us to the birds flying overhead, from the tiny creatures hurrying here and there near our feet to intimidating creatures of immense size, from an entire arena of things to humankind, which represents the hands, feet, eyes, ears, tongue, and lips of the tree of creation, in short, from everybody, every event, and every object, we get different messages; we try to decode them in our own way, enter deeper reveries as we succeed, open up more towards the essence, are further invigorated—how happy are those who can accomplish all this!—and then we can focus on the dimension that lies behind the apparent face of all things.

For such people, this universe and what it contains seems like a comprehensive book. This magical palace called the world becomes an exhibition of divine art. The life they lead turns into an enjoyable journey to the Hereafter and what they see and sense makes them realize that they are alive. And then they feel as if they were soaring past the horizons of the heart and spirit for a lifetime. As existence and what is beyond open to their consciousness, the knowledge and love of God within them transforms into a deeper love and attachment. Now these people feel Him in everything and relate every event and every object to Him. Life becomes more beautiful to them than ever before; everything changes its manner and language and assumes a more magical identity. Then their spirit, which ascends beyond all obvious considerations, awakens to deep secrets never unlocked before.

If we manage to overcome the barriers of the body and corporeality, we see the entire cosmos as if everything has passed to a different dimension and feel as if we are in a world of surprises. Then we interpret every event differently—the air we breath every moment; the rivers which flow chanting His Name, the blades of grass swaying sweetly as they offer bouquets of melodies to us, and the trees; the stars singing a new song to us every night; the moons and suns, whose rising and settings are all adjusted in precise measure and which offer us different feasts every night—and what is more, we feel as if everything is a part of our being because of the spaciousness faith brings to our hearts. And then every time we gaze at the magnificent spectacle of this cosmos, we let ourselves go into waterfalls of love and vitality and feel as if we are soaring through a magical time towards the reunion with the Most Beloved. As we walk, we benefit from the lights of the signs He placed on the road, we converse with everything living or non-living we encounter, give heartfelt greetings to the signs and sign bearers, try to transform the difficulties of travel into blessings of the way, make the hours, minutes, and seconds granted for our journey gain such depth that they become a means to reach eternity, and turn this transient life into a corridor leading to the realms beyond. Actually, all the beauties of this world which evoke surprise and admiration in hearts can only open up through our intentions and adjusting our perspective correctly, provided that the Beloved One looks upon us with mercy. Then these beauties become eternal, and a day comes when they rise on the horizons of our spirit and shine. We feel the genuine taste and delight of the fruits of life we enjoy thanks to the graces of the Beloved One. We understand the relation of other beings to us and the warm company they keep along the way by feeling and sensing their relation to the Only Beloved

One. And then, this relation within carries on as long as we manage to keep the warmth of our love, care, and closeness for Him, since all loves, cares, and relationships are for Him, who is the sole Ruler of the throne of love. Everything tells of Him in a different manner and style, utters words about Him to passersby, and whispers love of Him into our ears. So we love everything and everybody we come across on the way because of Him. If we are trying to keep our eyes on these roads, it is to see something from Him, and if we are alert to sounds, this is to hear something from Him. In fact, this is His right over us, and our responsibility toward Him. If a word is related to Him in the end, it may be considered to have found its value. Different considerations bear value if they can open a door to Him; and we can say that progress is being made if it is possible to keep every move and action within the scope of seeking His approval. We already know that we are sent into this world in order to prepare for a different realm. As for inviting to belief, it is nothing but calling people to such preparation. Those who believe in that are always aware in their feelings, thoughts, intentions, and all their actions that they are responding to that call, that they need to respond, and that they are on this testing ground and in this place of suffering in order to become worthy of the bounties and blessings beyond. So they constantly walk toward Him with the light of His presence in their eyes, the charm of believing in Him in their hearts, and a ceaseless desire for reunion in their dreams; by feeding their spirituality with faith, Islam, and perfect goodness,[37] by being immersed in knowledge of God, and being refined through love and zeal.... They are in a state of constant bliss, surprise and admiration. They listen to sounds belonging to Him along the way, ask everybody and everything they see they come across about Him. They walk toward that Eternal King of all the known and unknown realms, as if they are fixed on the target.

---

[37] The term *ihsan*, which is translated here as perfect goodness also denotes worshipping sincerely and seriously as if one were able to see God or at least in the awareness of being seen by Him.

They do not ask how long the road is, when the destination will be reached, or when the reunion will be realized; they do not wish for this journey of knowledge of God to end for they expect further graces and need more compassion. They are filled with considerations of loyalty and determination always to act sincerely, and eagerness for a wider perspective in their contemplation.

As they progress, they see better the smiling face of their fortune, the other side of their life, and the mysterious world of faith. Then they begin to draw new messages from everything, and they become more enthusiastic with every new sound and every glad tiding. They keep ascending as if realizing a holy Ascension (*miraj*). They reach levels previously unknown, travel through worlds unfamiliar to them, and greet everybody and everything they see. They shower all of these with smiles of contentment and walk toward the ultimate limits of the potential of their nature; smelling the roses and flowers on the way, talking with everything and everyone they encounter, conversing with light and shadow; listening to something of Him in every sound, every word, every accent, and every sight.

A time comes after this when they are always with Him, and they are freed of themselves. Their vision changes; they see the thorn as rose, and poison as honey... and they meet such great figures hidden behind humble appearances. God knows how many times they feel dizzy at different beauties, how many times their hearts thrill with divine surprises, how many chambers of secrets they visit, and how many times they receive divine compliments and graces in private. Every time they see and contemplate the different manifestations of His Beauty in different mirrors, the blood almost drains from their hearts, the rhythm of their pulse changes, and they sense Him alone. As a matter of fact, while our sensing Him is His due right, it is both a duty and blessing for us to do—or try to do—so. For the travelers who are aware of the gravity of this duty and who aim to attain the delight of this blessing, their journey is like a trip around the gardens of Paradise, no matter how steep and difficult the road being walked, and with the help of His

signs placed here and there, covering the seemingly impossible distances turns into a journey of joy and zeal; apparently impassable
chasms or obstacles are leapt over with the zest for reunion, and no
trace of fatigue from the way or from the troubles of walking is felt;
they wish to walk these paths forever. These souls, who are fixed on
reaching the Beloved and seeing Him, are aware that they continue
their lives by freeing themselves from the trivial matters of corporeality and the narrowness of the world, that they lead their lives
within the vast and colorful atlas of faith and knowledge of God
and are nourished by His graces. They revere everything they contemplate as a letter or a stamp from Him and always walk around
the limits of spiritual delights. They think every peak of knowledge
and love of God to be the ultimate citadel; they glorify Him with
"God is great," and express their gratitude with "all praise be to
God." However, they meet a new shower of surprises two steps later and find themselves in a different symphony of spiritual pleasures
and knowledge of God.

On every new peak they reach they sense the All-Beautiful One
in His different manifestations, they once more rise with love and
vitality and walk toward the next peak which lies further on. Beauties follow one another on the path they walk; neither the manifestations of His Beauty end, nor does the pleasure of contemplation
in their souls.

For those who can see and perceive, this road features love and
zeal, just as it is replete with reunion in the form of drops which
point to the ocean. God knows what else those who see the ocean
in the drop, who contemplate constellations in an atom witness
from the realms beyond, and what extraordinary sounds they listen
to, for, "*This world is but a mirror; nothing lasts but with the Almighty
Lord*" (anon). So, reading the signs is the purpose of creation and
the essential wisdom of being human.

A RADIANT MONTH IN A
DARKENING WORLD

The world is undergoing a series of depressions, one within the other. Humanity is restless and living with nightmares. Yet, Ramadan is once more on the way, appearing on the horizon like the silent full moon. Its light has started to diffuse the darkness of our horizon, and although it is only a temporary light, we feel relief in our souls.

No matter how much people are contaminated in thought and feeling, almost every Ramadan offers them, in some way, a bouquet of its charming holy light, purifying their hearts from dust and corrosion, illuminating them to their capacity and imbuing them with its own color. It removes all that befogs our horizons and flows into our hearts with its heavenly flavor and joy. Its light showers upon us like fireworks from the sky; it calms our unease and softens our harsh and aggressive thoughts. Almost every time Ramadan comes like tranquility descending from the sky, it comes among us with its heavenly color, allure, and dialect, making its magic felt in our souls. Each time we play host to Ramadan, this blessed month is so charming that it remains as fresh as the first time it came; its departure leaves us with longing.... We wait for a whole year for the days when it will return. Nevertheless, with the fasting, with the *iftar* and *sahur* meals, and the *tarawih* prayers,[38] there is always a feeling of familiarity. In this respect, neither does its arrival cause astonishment, nor its departure surprise; rather it has a heavenly side which can only be felt by our conscience. It is thanks to this as-

---

[38] *Iftar* is the fast-breaking meal at the sunset and *sahur* is the pre-dawn meal. *Tarawih* is a prayer special for Ramadan, which is observed voluntarily in the evening after *isha* prayer.

pect that Ramadan is able to distil our selves, purify our hearts, make our feelings keen, and tell us brand new things in a fresh language. Thanks to this aspect Ramadan never fades, loses color, or becomes dull; it does not tire its hosts either. On the contrary, it always comes like the spring and enwraps us gently, and then it goes away and leaves us with the feeling that autumn has arrived.

Almost every year, as it showers down upon our heads a mystery and an enchantment from the heavens, Ramadan makes itself felt with a new depth, each time with a new difference. Each and every time we find Ramadan to be different and more charming; we cherish a fervent love for it.

As a matter of fact when Ramadan comes, it plays through months and days, jumps through the seasons, and always arrives in a different manner; it embraces our hearts with the weather, the hue, and the patterns of the seasons: sometimes Ramadan pours its heavenly warmth into the bosom of the cold winter; sometimes it unites with the heat of summer and reminds us to use our will, playing on our determination, and directing our insights toward the horizon of spiritual life. Sometimes Ramadan lands like dew upon spring flowers and recites to us poems of revival. And sometimes it pierces through the gloom of the autumn with its heavenly joy; it takes us from the narrowness of worldliness to the spacious and relaxing climate of otherworldliness.

Like the rising and setting of the sun and the moon, we know when Ramadan will come by astronomic calculations. However, with each visit, Ramadan meets us with a variety of surprises and changes our lives completely. It reschedules the time we eat, drink, go to bed, and get up. It transforms us into spiritual beings in proportion to our capacity. And with its every aspect it speaks to our hearts about the faithfulness that is from beyond the heavens.

Almost every year when Ramadan comes, the heavens virtually descend upon the earth: the lights on the streets, the lamps surrounding the minarets and the Ramadan messages hanging between them, the fireworks flashing up here or there remind us of the stars and the meteors in the sky; the deep spiritual state of the believers in the mosque, who become finer and purer, who become innocent like angels, their vigilance, the way they start and break the fast all inspire us with the feeling that we are walking side by side with spiritual beings. This is true to such a degree that believers who are open to the horizon of the heart and spirituality experience a new feast with every pre-dawn meal; they overflow with a new exhilaration at every meal to break the fast, they observe every *tarawih* prayer with a new spiritual delight, and they frequently feel as if they are in a world of dreams. This blessed month is constantly enwrapped with divine forgiveness; it promises the same to those who live in its atmosphere and it has a different influence on every person who has some degree of religious belief: it changes the limits of a believer's heart with its own peculiar charm, reflecting its own hue in their nature, and openly or not, it makes those who believe with all their heart aware of the mystery of the realms beyond, paving the way for people to surpass their corporeality and to become almost different beings.

With the coming of Ramadan, otherworldly whispers are heard to emanate from human emotions. The sense of the realms beyond spreads throughout everything, like the most beautiful of scents. Through an entire month this blessed piece of time presents us with its deepest silent poems; faith and worship are the basic components of these silent poems, and they go hand in hand, presenting us with magical horizons that transcend the fields of the sciences; we never have enough of gazing at them.

Just as the sun reaches everything on earth to a certain degree and its rays reflect on every object at different frequencies, so too in the month of Ramadan are the worlds beyond the heavens presented in different interactions with the earth and its inhabitants, particularly with the hearts of the believers. Pure spiritual realms everywhere emanate a spirit, a meaning, a spell that far overshadow sunlight; it manifests its own depths in those hearts which are open to the divine and inspires them with depth of faith. In this way, this world and the other almost come together, side by side; worship flows from this world to the other, whereas goodness and blessings flow from the other one to this. This state triggers profound dreams and feelings in us, making us realize that nothing in the world can be so beautiful or fascinating. Sometimes, as the sounds in the mosques intermingle with the lights, and pour down our heads, everyone feels in such a state that we never desire to leave that magical atmosphere. Even if we leave, our hearts always remain in rhythm with what goes on there.

In Ramadan we feel the joy of a celebration every day. We are aware of its warmth on our journeys between work, home, and mosque. We feel it when we plunge into the dreams that open up to otherworldliness. Sometimes we run to the mosque, striving to overcome our distance from our Lord. We strengthen our wishes for goodness by praying, and we try to be cleansed from spiritual dirt by repentance and taking refuge in God. Day and night we value our place in the divine presence as yet another chance of purification, and we change the color of life. In this way our life ceases to be an unsolved riddle; it turns into a beauty of which we can never have enough. It is inhaled, felt, and becomes a pleasure that pours into us.

And the call to prayer resounding throughout the neighborhood and the sound of the glorification of God from the mosques, the fascinating spiritual aura there, the special language of the *tarawih* prayers, observed by both men and women, young and old, by all Muslims; all these elevate Ramadan to such an inimitable level that those who feel and observe Ramadan thoroughly savor all the different thoughts as if they were all side by side with the inhabitants of heavens; they are enraptured. Sometimes in Ramadan—the ability to sense it depends on the spiritual depth of the individual—such a deep otherworldliness enwraps one that, while listening to the voices rising from the minarets one feels as if it is Bilal, the Prophet's muezzin, calling; the imam is seen as a privileged person who has the title of God's vicegerent, and the people around one are perceived as the blessed Companions who were honored with seeing the Prophet. The excitement completely penetrates people who feel like this, they cannot hold back their tears, and they feel as if they are just one step away from the gates of Paradise.

JALAL AL-DIN RUMI

There are some significant personalities who with the help of their voice and breath, their love and excitement, and their promise for humanity always remain fresh and alive over the course of centuries. Time evidently fails to make these characters obsolete. Their thoughts, analyses, explanations, and spiritual messages, which never will be lost, represent ever new, alternative solutions and prescriptions for today's social problems, in great variety and diversity.

Rumi is one such personality. Despite the centuries that separate his life from ours, Rumi continues to hear and to listen to us, to share our feelings, to present solutions to our problems in a voice that is without equal. Despite the fact that he lived some seven centuries ago, he remains absolutely alive among and with us today. He is a man of light—one who receives his light from the spirit of the Master of Humanity (Prophet Muhammad, peace and blessings be upon him), distributing this light in various ways to just about everywhere. He was chosen to be one of the world's saints and to be pure of heart; a blessed one whose words are outstanding among those heroes of love and passion. He was and continues to function as Israfil, blowing life into dead spirits. He continues to provide the water of life to the barren hearts of many, a spiritual irrigation. He continues to provide light for the travelers on their paths. He was and continues to be the perfect heir of the Prophet.

Jalal al-Din Rumi, a man of God. He hastened toward God on his own spiritual journey, and in addition to this, he evoked similar journeys in countless others—journeys marked by an eager striving toward God. He was a balanced man of ecstasy who sprang alive with love and excitement; he did this to such an extent that he inspired in others these significant feelings, and he continues to do so. In addition to his passion for God and along with his knowledge and love of Him, Rumi further is renowned as a hero in terms of both his respect and fear of God. He was and continues to be one who beckons, one whose powerful voice invites everyone to the truth and the ultimate blessed reality. Rumi was an inclusive master whose joy was a direct consequence of His joy, whose love and passion were the result of His special favors to Rumi. His life provides real evidence of the Truth. While he spoke to those of his own times in an effective manner, Rumi has become even more influential in that he made his voice and breath, which reflected the voice and breath of Prophet Muhammad, peace be upon him, continue to be heard for centuries after. He spoke with such an enchanting voice that he was able to guide not only his blessed contemporaries, but also people of our time, centuries removed from his physical existence. God bestowed upon him this important duty. For this purpose, God blessed him with impeccable inner and outer qualities so that he would prove successful in this undertaking. His heart was full of the Divine Light. As such, his essence is marked by his wisdom, which shines like a light reflected through a precious gem. His innermost self was enveloped with Divine mysteries. His inner eyes were enlightened by this special light.

On this horizon, Jalal al-Din Rumi represents the North Star, the heart of the circle of guidance for his time. He embodies the characteristics of the lamp of sainthood, taking its light from that of the truth of the Prophet. Many of God's blessed creatures are instinctively attracted to light. Rumi's light has attracted hundreds of thousands of spiritual butterflies; they are drawn to the light. He represents a guide for humanity's quest for the perfection of human qualities. Rumi was a careful exegete of the truths presented in the Qur'an. A fluent interpreter of love and zeal for Prophet Muhammad, peace be upon him, Rumi was able to use a mysterious language to guide others to a love of God. Those who enter his sphere are able to reach an ultimate sense or feeling in the presence of God.

Those who examined the Qur'an by his guideposts underwent changes (and continue to undergo changes) similar to those witnessed by the people who lived in the era of the Prophet himself. When the verses of the Qur'an were interpreted by Rumi's closest associates, all hearts benefited from the illumination provided by his wisdom; it was as if all of heaven's mysteries were opened by his wholehearted recitation of that one word—God.

Rumi's love for God was a fiery one, with a constant longing for the mysteries of God. He experienced love and passion both in his solitary asceticism and his activities in the community. It was in his solitariness that he became most open to the truest union with God, and it was during separation from all things except God that his heart burned with fire. And while such a sense of burning would prove difficult for many to bear, Rumi never showed any signs of discontent. Rather, such burning was considered a requirement for passion, and refraining from complaint was seen to be in the tradition of loyalty. For Rumi, those who profess a love of God necessarily must accompany their statement of "I love" with a sense of furious burning—this is the price one willingly must pay for being close to or in union with God. Additionally, one must engage in behavior that is to a large extent ascetic, such as moderate eating, drinking, sleeping, and a constant awareness and orientation toward God in one's speech, and one inevitably must experience bewilderment when endowed with God's bounties.

Rumi cannot understand how a lover can sleep in an immoderate way, as it takes away from the time that can be shared with the Beloved. For him, excessive sleep is offensive to the Beloved. As God instructed David, saying, *"O David, those who indulge in sleep without contemplating Me and then claim to be in love are liars,"* so too did Rumi state, *"When the darkness falls, lovers become intense."* Rumi continually recommended this not only in words, but also in his actions.

The following quotation from his *Divan-i Kabir* best represents several droplets from the ocean of his feelings and excitement, erupting like a volcano:

I am like Majnun[39] in my poor heart, which is without limbs, because I have no strength to contest the love of God. Every day and night I continue in my efforts to free myself from the bonds of the chain of love; a chain that keeps me imprisoned. When the dream of the Beloved begins I find myself in blood. Because I am not fully conscious, I am afraid in that I may paint Him with the blood of my heart. In fact, You, O Beloved, must ask the fairies; they know how I have burned through the night. Everyone has gone to sleep. But I, the one who has given his heart to You, do not know sleep like them. Throughout the night, my eyes look at the sky, counting the stars. His love so profoundly took my sleep that I do not really believe it ever will come back.

If the spirit of the anthology of Rumi's poems—which are the essence of love, passion, divine presence, and excitement—were to be wrung out, the result would be cries of love, longing, and hope. Throughout his life Rumi expressed love, and in turn, he believed he was beloved because of this. Accordingly, he spoke of his love and relationship with Him. When he did so, he was not alone—he took along with him many blessed individuals who were his audience. He assumed it to be a requisite of loyalty to offer, cup by cup, the drinks presented to him on the heavenly table to others who were in his circle of light.

Thus, the following quotation represents the ambiguous chanting that is reflected in his heavenly travels:

> The Buraq[40] of love has taken my mind as well as my heart, do not ask me where.
> I have reached such a realm that there is no moon, nor day.
> I have reached a world where the world is no longer the world.

Rumi's spiritual journey was an ascension in the shadow of the Ascension of the Prophet, which is described by Süleyman Chelebi (the author of the Turkish Mevlid—recited in commemoration of

---

39 Majnun is a legendary personality of love found in Sufi literature.
40 Buraq is the name of the horse that carried Prophet Muhammad, peace be upon him, during his Ascension into Heaven.

the birth of the Prophet)—in these words: *"There was no space, Earth, or heavens."* What his soul heard and watched was a special reflection of His courtesy, which cannot be seen by the eyes, heard by the ears, or comprehended by one's mind or thought. Such reflections are not attainable by all. Rumi spiritually ascended, and he saw, tasted, and knew all that was possible for a mortal being. Those who do not see cannot know. Those who do not taste cannot feel. Those who are capable of feeling in this manner generally do not divulge the secrets that they have attained. And those who do reveal these secrets often find them to be above the level of the comprehension of most people. As the famous Turkish poet Shaykh Ghalib said, *"The Beloved's candle has such a wonderful light, and its light does not fit into the lamp glass of Heaven."*

The love, relationship, and warmth toward all creation expressed by Rumi are a projection of a deeply-rooted divine love. Rumi, whose nature was intoxicated by the cup of love, embraced all of creation with a projection of that love. He was involved in a dialogue with every creature, and all this was a result of nothing but his deep love of God and his relationship with the Beloved.

I believe that these disordered and somewhat confused explanations are far from adequate to describe Rumi. This disorder is an inevitable result of my search for a relationship with him. A droplet cannot describe the ocean, nor can an atom describe the sun. Even so, since his light falls once again on this earth, I would like to say, in a few sentences, some words about Jalal al-Din Rumi.

Rumi was born in the city of Balkh in 1207, at a time when all of Asia was suffering from social, political, and military problems. His father, Muhammad Baha al-Din al-Siddiqi, was in the tenth generation of the descendants of Abu Bakr al-Siddiq, the first caliph of Islam. According to Tahir al-Mevlevi, Rumi's mother was also a descendant of the Prophet. He was the blessed fruit of a hallowed family tree. Being known as the Sultan al-Ulama (the Leader of Scholars), his father was a man of truth and an heir of the Prophet. Like many friends of God, he was persecuted and eventually compelled to migrate. Accordingly, he left the land of Khawarzm, where he was born, and undertook a lengthy journey that encompassed various destinations. First, he and his family visited the Holy Land, the cities of Mecca and Medina. From there, he traveled and remained for some time in Damascus, where he met many pious persons, such as Ibn al-'Arabi, and exchanged spiritual enlightenment with them.

Accompanying his father, the young Rumi, six or seven years of age, witnessed these and other events; his inquisitive senses enabled him to experience all of these with remarkable clarity. The young Rumi understood his environment even at such a tender age, and he was able to penetrate into the secret world of Ibn al-'Arabi. As an endowment of his presence with Ibn al-'Arabi, the child received kindness and favors. Despite the unfortunate circumstances surrounding their migration and the many difficulties that accompanied them, the family's journey provided them with a variety of favors and inspiration. Like Abraham, Moses, and the Prophet of Islam, may God's blessings be upon all of them, Rumi was able continuously to find these blessings and favors. Welcoming what fate gave him, he became a receiver of numerous bounties provided by God. The journey took this blessed family to the city of Erzincan, and later to Karaman. It was during his time in the latter city that Rumi studied, for a short period, in the Halawiyye madrasa. In addition to this school, he studied Islamic sciences in several religious schools in Damascus and Aleppo. After graduating, he returned to the city of Konya, which he considered his hometown and a place of special regard. It was there that he married Gevher Khatun, the daughter of Shams al-Din Samarqandi. After some time, Rumi's father, Sultan al-Ulama, died and returned to God. Under the supervision of Burhan al-Din al-Tirmidhi, Rumi began his long spiritual journey. After several years, at the suggestion of Rukn al-Din Zarqubi, Rumi met with Shams-i Tabrizi, who was then on a visit to Konya. It was through his meeting with Shams that he furthered his spiritual journey and eventually developed into the person who now is known the world over for his spiritual depth. What has been mentioned so far, in fact, represents an attempt to open a few small windows on the life of an exceptional personality in this creation, one whose capacity is open to the lofty world. This is also an attempt to present the life of an important representative of the Muhammadi spirit (i.e., the practice of the sunna)—displaying several snapshots of a man determined to dedicate his existence to the afterlife. It is not my intention to stir the waters that comprise the lives of such remarkable and pure personalities with debates and questions that ultimately only will agitate and obscure. However, one must wonder whether Rumi opened the horizon of Shams or whether Shams took Rumi to the world of the unseen. Who took whom to the reality of realities—the peak of love and joy? Who directed whom to the real Besought and the real Beloved? Answering these questions is beyond the capacity of most ordinary people. One can say, at least, the following: During this period of time, two skillful and acute spirits came together, like two oceans merging into one another. By sharing the divine bounties and gifts received from their Lord, they both reached peaks that most people would not be able to reach easily on their own account.

Through their spiritual cooperation, they established camps on the peaks of knowledge, love, compassion, and joy for God. As much as they enlightened those of their own times, they also influenced all centuries to follow, an effect that is still present today. The spring of sweet water that they represent continues to nourish the thirsty. They have been remembered continuously over the centuries for their beautiful contributions to countless lives. Here it is important to note that Rumi was informed by numerous sources in the flow of ideas, including his father, the great master of scholars. During his journey, he seemed to have left many of his contemporaries behind. His love and compassion flowed like the waters of the world's oceans, so much so that while continuing to live physically among humans, he managed to become ever closer to God. It seems he never elevated himself above others except through his writings, both during his life and after entering eternity; he provides a guiding star that echoes the spiritual life of the Prophet of Islam. Accordingly, he is among the few people who have exerted a great influence through both space and time.

Rumi, the Master, was not a pupil, a dervish, a representative, or master as is known among traditional Sufis. He developed a new method that was colored with revivalism and personal, independent reasoning by taking the Qur'an, the sunna, and Islamic piety as his points of reference. With a new voice and breath, he successfully brought to a new divine table both those of his generation and those of later times. As far as his relationship with God is concerned, he was a man of love and passion. As for those who turn to him for the sake of God, he represents a compassionate bearer of God's divine cup of love. Yes, as the rains of mercy fall forth from the clouds of the sky, and if the collections of his poems were to be wrung out, God's love and the love of His Messenger would gush forth in showers. His *Mesnevi*, exuberant with his spirit, a book that is in part didactic and was put in book form by his disciple, Husam al-Din Chelebi, represents his largest, most monumental treatise. While it stems from his involvement with the floods of a high level love and passion, it was presented in smaller waves so that their essence might be understood by a larger part of humanity who did not share the same capacity. His other work, *Divan-i Kabir*, is both informed by and presented in this higher level of love and passion and better represents his own abilities.

In the *Mesnevi*, feelings and thoughts are put in such a way that they do not confuse our intelligence and in such a style that it does not surpass our understanding. As for the *Divan-i Kabir*, everything is like an erupting volcano. Its meaning is not understood easily by most. A careful investigation will show that this great book of Rumi's thought will explain such concepts as *baqa billah maallah* (to live by God with God) and *fana fillah* (annihilation in God) in the context of a larger understanding of the world of the unseen. Those who are capable of realizing this excitement in Rumi's Divan will find themselves in extreme bewilderment before a flood of love and ecstasy that is comparable to volcanic eruption. In these poems of the master, which are not easily accessible for most people, the limits of reason are surpassed, the meanings of the poems are elevated above the norms for humanity, and the eternal nature of the unseen world shadows the ephemeral colors and forms of what one encounters in their physical being.

Jalal al-Din Rumi was nourished by the fruit of numerous sources of ideas, including religious seminaries, Sufi lodges, and Sufi hermitages associated with strict Sufi asceticism. Rumi attained an understanding of the Ultimate Reality. He cultivated the heavenly through his own methods. Eventually, he became a central star, the North Star, in the sky which houses sainthood. He was like a bright moon that rotates on its own axis. He was a hero who reached the places where he should have reached and stopped where he should have stopped. He read carefully what he saw and evaluated well what he felt. He never displayed or participated in any improper behavior during his journey to God. Even though the numbers were vast, Rumi never lost any of the bountiful gifts he received from the world of the unseen, not even to the weight of an atom. Like many of his predecessors, he voiced these divine bounties through his poetry in an impressive manner. He often voiced his love and excitement in seemingly magical words that resembled the finest of precious gems. Within the vagueness of the poetry, he mastered the art of explaining his ambiguous statements in ways that opened their meaning to friends, but remained obscured to outsiders.

These statements that were at times both clear and ambiguous are the voice and breath of his own horizon—he was not acquainted with other pens or the wells of ink which supplied them. Although one can find a few foreign words or works falsely attributed to him, Rumi's anthology represents a warmth, the music of his own heart, a music that brings all who hear it under its influence with a captivating control.

Rumi possessed a very delicate disposition, often appearing more compassionate than a mother to her child. In short, he was an exceptional personality, particularly in his projection of the spirit of God's Messenger in his own time. This is illustrated in his collected works, including the *Mesnevi*, *Divan-i Kabir*, some collected letters associated with familial relations, and his special behavior with friends. Those who witnessed this were greatly excited to see the perfect heir of the Prophet and would say with great humility and respect, *"This is a grace from God. He gives it to whom He wants"* (Maeda 5:54).

Rumi was a man of genuine sincerity and loyalty. He lived by what he felt in his heart as long as it did not contradict the teachings and laws of religion. While making his faith the focus of his life, while showing others the way of life, while blowing into the *ney*, and while dancing like a butterfly, his heart was burning with love and longing; it always ached and sang like the plaintive *ney*. Those who were not aching could not understand him. Those who were rude and tactless could not feel what he felt. He said, "I want a heart that is split, part by part, because of the pain of separation from God, so that I might explain my longing and complaint to it." Saying this, he searched for friends who had similar longings and complaints.

Throughout his life Rumi witnessed and experienced many difficulties. Yet, he never acted in a harsh manner or tried to hurt others in response. While proclaiming the bounties of God, Rumi roared and was fearless. In his personal engagements, he was always meek and humble, willing and ready to embrace everyone with great compassion. Bad characteristics, such as selfishness, pretentiousness, arrogance, or aggressiveness, found no quarter with him; they could not even come close. He was extremely respectful to all, especially those with whom he had the closest associations: he referred to his friend, Shams-i Tabrizi, the man from whom he lit his own candle, as his "Master"; he called his pupil and spiritual representative, Salah al-Din Faridun, "Spiritual Leader," "Master," and "Sultan"; he always mentioned Husam al-Din Chelebi with great respect. His behavior toward his family members mirrored the behavior of the Prophet toward his own family. His community of followers was open to everyone—like that of the Prophet—and he was close to even those who were farthest from him, so much so that his greatest enemies were compelled, unwillingly, to throw themselves upon his compassionate embrace. Once having entered this circle, no one ever abandoned him.

On the one hand, Rumi, the Master, had a specific intimate relationship with the world of the unseen, but on the other hand, especially as far as his relationship with people was concerned, he never promoted any sense that he was greatly different; this was because of his utmost sincerity and humility. He lived among the people as one of them. He would listen to them, eat and drink with them; he never would disclose the secrets cultivated between him and God to those who could not truly appreciate their value. Being a guide, he lived by what he believed and always tried to find a way to penetrate the hearts of those around him. He would call his gatherings "Talks on the Beloved," thus making an effort constantly to draw attention to Him. He would say, "Love," "Longing," "Ecstasy," and "Attraction" to try to share with others the gushing excitement and feelings that were inherent in his spirit. He would show everyone who passed within his sphere the horizon of real humanity. He never allowed his eyes to rest on worldly possessions but rather would distribute any accumulated possession or any money that was beyond his own needs among those who were in need. When food was scarce in his house, he would say, "Thank God as today our house resembles the Prophet's house." Accordingly, it was through thankfulness and patience that he made his spiritual flights into the world beyond. Rumi did not accept charity or alms; in this way he was able to avoid a feeling of indebtedness—he suffered from hunger, lived modestly, and yet never would let others be aware of such situations. He did not want to stain his service of guidance for God by accepting gifts or presents.

In addition to his ascetic life, his fear of God, his chastity, his divine protection from sinfulness, his self-sufficiency, and his pure life that was directed toward the world of the unseen, Rumi's knowledge of God, his love of God, and his utmost longing for God kept him, throughout his life, rising as one of the moons that illuminates the sky of sainthood. His love for God was one that surpassed the normal bounds of love—it was a transcendental love. He thoroughly believed that he was also loved by Him. This security did not result, for him, in losses—neither in a lack of fear nor in a loss of respect for God. This was the horizon of faith and accountability, and Rumi would hint at this balance between fear and hope as an expression of the bounties offered by God. We rightly can call this sense of balance "The Declarer of the Gifts of the Eternal Sultan."

In his inner world, the various waterfalls of love flowed out at a variety of volumes and distances. His sincere approach toward the Divine and his fidelity were rewarded with divine ecstasy and attractions. He was privileged with the greatest closeness to God, and he frequently sipped from the cup of divine love, cup by cup, becoming intoxicated. He wanted to see, to know, to feel, and to speak only of Him and to relate all of his work and words only to Him. He was so earnest in this regard that if his eyes turned to outsiders for even a brief moment, he would sit and cry a great many tears. He strongly desired to live in the spacious environment of togetherness with Him. He convulsively struggled to be both a lover and a beloved and spent the minutes of his life in an intoxication that emanated from both.

Many were the lovers who felt these spiritual joys in a similar way and preceded Rumi in life and death. Yet Rumi's superiority is revealed by the way in which he spoke out so courageously about his feelings and thoughts in his *Divan-i Kabir*. In fact, since the time of the Prophet and through the periods that followed, there have been many great heroes who have been afforded superiority over Rumi by common consensus. However, Rumi's superiority lies in a special merit, whereas theirs are more general merits. Therefore, in this regard we can perceive Rumi as the leader of this field, the finest among the fine. Rumi is an outstanding guide in leading people to the Most Beautiful of the beautiful on the path of love.

It is a lofty rank for a human to be able to love God from the depth of his heart and always to remember Him with deep love and passion. If there is a higher rank than this, it is the awareness of the fact that all love, longing, ecstasy, and attraction in human beings are the result of His kind treatment and favor. Rumi breathed God's Beautiful Names and Attributes every time he inhaled and exhaled. He was aware that his disposition was a direct result of the grace and favor bestowed upon him by God. Those whose horizon fails to achieve this unique level may not be able to understand this. According to the following anonymous poem, there is no doubt that just as words represent the shells of meanings encompassed within, the abilities and capacities of humans are simply factors and conditions that are invitations for the receiving of divine gifts and:

> *The works of His grace are based on the ability of creatures.*
> *From the rain of April, a snake makes poison,*
> *While an oyster makes a pearl.*

INDEX